Guilt

This insightful and innovative book sheds light on the complexity of the concept of guilt, while exploring aspects of guilt that have previously been overlooked in psychoanalytic theory and discourse.

Offering original insights on the topic, Donald L. Carveth looks at Freud's failure to distinguish persecutory guilt from reparative guilt, and the superego from the conscience. The significance of these distinctions for both psychosocial theory and clinical practice is explored throughout the volume. Carveth distinguishes varieties of punitive guilt, such as justified, unjustified, "borrowed" or induced, existential and collective. He expertly describes patterns of self-punishment and self-sabotage, while also addressing the widespread use of persecutory guilt and self-punishment as a defence against and evasion of reparative guilt, contrition, and reparation. Throughout the volume, Carveth critically reviews a range of recent contributions to psychoanalytic literature to support his theories.

Part of the Routledge Introductions to Contemporary Psychoanalysis series, this book will be of interest to psychoanalysts, psychotherapists, social scientists, and social philosophers, as well as to those studying ethics and theology.

Donald L. Carveth is an emeritus professor of sociology and social and political thought and a senior scholar at York University, Toronto, Canada. He is a past director of the Toronto Institute of Psychoanalysis and a past editor-in-chief of the *Canadian Journal of Psychoanalysis/Revue Canadienne de Psychanalyse*. He is the author of *Psychoanalytic Thinking* (2018) and *The Still Small Voice* (2013).

Routledge Introductions to Contemporary Psychoanalysis

Aner Govrin, Ph.D.
Series Editor

Tair Caspi, Ph.D.
Executive Editor

Yael Peri Herzovich
Assistant Editor

"Routledge Introductions to Contemporary Psychoanalysis" is one of the prominent psychoanalytic publishing ventures of our day. It will comprise dozens of books that will serve as concise introductions dedicated to influential concepts, theories, leading figures, and techniques in psychoanalysis covering every important aspect of psychoanalysis.

The length of each book is fixed at 40,000 words.

The series' books are designed to be easily accessible to provide informative answers in various areas of psychoanalytic thought. Each book will provide updated ideas on topics relevant to contemporary psychoanalysis – from the unconscious and dreams, projective identification and eating disorders, through neuropsychoanalysis, colonialism, and spiritual-sensitive psychoanalysis. Books will also be dedicated to prominent figures in the field, such as Melanie Klein, Jacques Lacan, Sándor Ferenczi, Otto Kernberg, and Michael Eigen.

Not serving solely as an introduction for beginners, the purpose of the series is to offer compendiums of information on particular topics within different psychoanalytic schools. We ask authors to review a topic but also address the readers with their own personal views and contribution to the specific chosen field. Books will make intricate ideas comprehensible without compromising their complexity.

We aim to make contemporary psychoanalysis more accessible to both clinicians and the general educated public.

Aner Govrin – Editor

Donald Meltzer
A Contemporary Introduction
Meg Harris Williams

Projective Identification
A Contemporary Introduction
Robert Waska

Transgender Identities
A Contemporary Introduction
Alessandra Lemma

Sándor Ferenczi
A Contemporary Introduction
Alberto Fergusson and Miguel Gutierrez-Pelaez

Christopher Bollas
A Contemporary Introduction
Steve Jaron

Eating Disorders
A Contemporary Introduction
Tom Wooldridge

Michael Eigen
A Contemporary Introduction
Loray Daws

Psychoanalytic Field Theory
A Contemporary Introduction
Giuseppe Civitarese

Psychoanalysis and Colonialism
A Contemporary Introduction
Sally Swartz

W.R. Bion's Theories of Mind
A Contemporary Introduction
Annie Reiner

Herbert Rosenfeld
A Contemporary Introduction
Robert Hinshelwood

Neuropsychoanalysis
A Contemporary Introduction
Georg Northoff

Spiritually-Sensitive Psychoanalysis
A Contemporary Introduction
Gideon Lev

Psychoanalysis and Homosexuality
A Contemporary Introduction
Leezah Hertzmann and Juliet Newbigin

Melanie Klein
A Contemporary Introduction
Penelope Garvey

The Unconscious
A Contemporary Introduction
Joseph Newirth

Guilt
A Contemporary Introduction
Donald L. Carveth

Guilt

A Contemporary Introduction

Donald L. Carveth

Routledge
Taylor & Francis Group

LONDON AND NEW YORK

Designed cover image: Cover image © Michal Heiman, *Asylum 1855–2020, The Sleeper* (video, psychoanalytic sofa and Plate 34), exhibition view, Herzliya Museum of Contemporary Art, 2017

First published 2024
by Routledge
4 Park Square, Milton Park, Abingdon, Oxon OX14 4RN

and by Routledge
605 Third Avenue, New York, NY 10158

Routledge is an imprint of the Taylor & Francis Group, an informa business

British Library Cataloguing-in-Publication Data
A catalogue record for this book is available from the British Library

ISBN: 978-1-032-38930-1 (hbk)
ISBN: 978-1-032-38266-1 (pbk)
ISBN: 978-1-003-34751-4 (ebk)

DOI: 10.4324/9781003347514

Typeset in Times New Roman
by Apex CoVantage, LLC

Jeanie

Contents

Preface   *xi*

1 Guilt   1

2 Conscience   7

3 Guilt evasion in the self, society,
   and psychoanalysis   11

4 Conscience vs. superego   21

5 Two case vignettes   35

6 Recent contributions to the theory of
   the superego, guilt, and conscience   39

7 Why I write about guilt   65

   References   *69*
   Index   *77*

Let wickedness escape as it may at the bar, it never fails of doing justice upon itself, for every guilty person is his own hangman.

– Seneca

Preface

Although I originally trained as a sociologist, my pre-existing interest in Freud made it impossible for me to accept socially determinist theories of the self. Thanks to the work of Dennis H. Wrong (1961) I was able to write a doctoral dissertation elaborating on his critique of "the oversocialized conception of man in modern sociology." At the same time my sociological training and my interest in existentialism and the humanistic psychosocial perspective of Erich Fromm (1947) made equally unacceptable the "undersocialized" conception of personality that found the forces resisting socialization primarily in Freud's somatically grounded drives of sex and aggression (Carveth, 1984a).

Here began my evolution toward the dialectical thinking (Carveth, 2018) that seeks to subsume and yet transcend both nature and nurture, biological and environmental determinants, and include a measure of agency and responsibility in psychosocial science, the study of the human subject/object. Such dialectical thinking can be found in the recently revived thought of Erich Fromm (Carveth, 2017; McGlaughlin, 2023) and in the critique of bipolarity in theory and in practice, in therapeutic work on the (all-good/all-bad) splitting we encounter in ourselves, in our patients, in psychoanalysis itself, and in the socio-cultural milieu that surrounds and shapes us.

In much of the revisionist psychoanalysis that emerged over the past half-century, the evasion of guilt and both the superego and the conscience, the psychic regulators that generate it, is evident. These theoretical developments (in my view, regressions) in the microcosm of psychoanalysis are paralleled in the socio-political macrocosm by the unrelenting attack on regulation and regulators that characterize neoliberalism and market fundamentalism. These forces on the right have gone a long way toward the dismantlement of the social state. Ironically, they have recently been joined by forces on what I think of as the pseudo-left, whose attack on regulation has taken the form of demanding not only to "defund the police" but also to "cancel" any authority that would presume to defend free speech. Just as "the narcissistic personality of our time" (Lasch, 1979) recognizes no limits, so law enforcement and even the law itself is flouted on both the (pseudo) left and the right, and even in the highest offices in the land.

A major reason for our moral confusion in both society and psychoanalysis is the failure to recognize the existence of a conscience apart from the moralistic, socially constructed superego (Sagan, 1988; Carveth, 2013). Taught to maintain neutrality and refrain from being judgmental or "superego-ish" with patients, without a concept of a conscience distinct from superego (either a separate mental structure or a prosocial, as distinct from the antisocial, part of the id), theory succumbs to the colonization of morality by the superego, and clinicians fall victim to moral relativism. Without a conscience separate from the superego, we have no judge to judge the judge. If with Strachey (1934) we feel the patient's superego ought to be modified, we lack any principled basis for determining in what directions.

Without the distinction between the superego and conscience, justified critique of authoritarianism can itself become unconscionably authoritarian (viz., the opposition to those refusing COVID-19 vaccination or organizing protests against it). At the same time, "woke" liberals are defenceless against authoritarians attacking free speech "under the banner of the superego" because they know no higher moral principle (conscience) from which to call them out. It is well to recall in this connection that memorable moment when Joe McCarthy's superegoic attacks were denounced as unconscionable by Joseph Welch: "Let us not assassinate this lad further, Senator. You have done enough. Have you no sense of decency?" (U.S. Senate Archive, June 9, 1954).

This book is dedicated to the clarification of our confusion in both psychoanalysis and society in general with respect to guilt (failing to distinguish persecutory and reparative), superego (failing to distinguish it from conscience), and what ultimately generates justified guilt: namely, human destructiveness or evil.

Except for the seriously psychopathic, in order to act, most people have to convince themselves that what they are about to do is, for the most part, good. In order to do evil, most people have to convince themselves that it is not evil but good.

In order to feel guilt, evildoers first have to change their minds about what they have done, seeing it not as good but as wrong, bad, or evil. Without such a change of mind, such a revised definition of the situation, people are unable to feel guilt, remorse, or regret and, hence, they are unable to repent and mourn their destructiveness.

In seeking to understand evil Kennedy (2022) emphasizes the role of an "evil moral climate" or an "evil imagination." He points out how the BBC research that followed up on Milgram's (1963) work on obedience showed that participants came to believe that their actions were serving a worthy purpose. Likewise, Kennedy points out that "people in early modern England sincerely believed that the civilizing mission was a moral obligation, and that it was good to bring people from a state of barbarism to a civilized way of life" (ch. 5).

In his study, *The Nazi Doctors*, Robert Lifton (1986) found that they were, for the most part, not psychopaths but dedicated physicians working hard to cut out the cancer that, in their racist ideology, they associated with the Jews.

Because in psychoanalysis we have associated the antisocial with the id and the prosocial with the superego, it has been difficult for us to see evil as superego-driven. The point I want to emphasize is that the greater part of human evil is done not by "do-badders" but by "do-gooders." Those who planned and carried out the atomic bombing of Hiroshima and Nagasaki were not psychopaths but people who believed in the righteousness of their cause – as were those who flew airplanes into the World Trade Center.

The belief that our cause is righteous and that God is on our side is the root of much human evil. Most evildoers have good intentions. They may often be found "marching under the banner of the superego."

While the superego sometimes defends against barbarism, as Freud (1930) thought (at least in his sociological as distinct from his clinical writings), it frequently encourages it and gives barbarism its blessing.

Chapter 1 describes the nature and varieties of guilt.

Chapter 2 concerns conscience and the controversies surrounding this concept.

Chapter 3 discusses guilt evasion in the self, society, and psychoanalysis, including self-punishment (persecutory guilt) inflicted by the superego as a defence against the mature (reparative) guilt generated by conscience.

Chapter 4 emphasizes the differences between the superego and the conscience and the conflicts between them.

Chapter 5 presents two case vignettes that illustrate the clinical relevance of these concepts.

Chapter 6 critically reviews some of the more recent literature on guilt and the superego.

Chapter 7 argues guilt is a fundamental feature of human existence and a central topic of psychoanalytic concern.

Chapter 1

Guilt

Defined legally, guilt is the state of having violated a law; defined morally, it is the state of having transgressed a moral norm. In *The Genealogy of Morals* (Second Essay, "Guilt, Bad Conscience, and Related Matters") Nietzsche (1887) writes:

> Have these genealogists of morality up to now allowed themselves to dream, even remotely, that, for instance, that major moral principle "guilt" *[Schuld]* derived its origin from the very materialistic idea "debt" *[Schulden]*? Or that punishment developed as a *repayment*?

Former prisoners who have completed their sentences are said to have "paid their debt" to society.

Legal or metaphysical guilt and psychological or experiential guilt need not correspond. It is not rare for people judged to *be* guilty not to *feel* guilty. And sometimes people *feel* guilty though no one (other than themselves, on some level of consciousness) has so judged them. There is no necessary coincidence between legal or moral guilt and psychological guilt. Such discrepancies may arise from varying circumstances. For example, I have been judged guilty, but I believe myself to be innocent and therefore do not feel guilty. Alternatively, I have been judged guilty, but I believe the laws or moral norms that have been applied are invalid or unjust. Commonly, psychopathic people are thought to have no capacity to feel guilt, but I have argued (Carveth, 2007) they

DOI: 10.4324/9781003347514-1

are merely skilled in the arts of silencing both their superego and their conscience.

Sometimes I may judge myself guilty and feel guilty even though no one else has so judged me. This may be due to my feeling that the laws or norms by which others judge me are too lax, or because they are not aware of my sins or crimes. When people feel guilty despite being unaware of having committed any crimes or sins, psychoanalysts posit the operation of an unconscious judge that is aware of the real or imagined transgressions and is punishing them with guilt (Freud, 1923, 1930).

Sometimes people are conscious of feeling guilt but unaware of its grounds. At other times, they are unaware that they are feeling guilty, feeling something else instead. Freud (1930) writes that

> it is very conceivable that the sense of guilt . . . is not perceived as such . . . and remains to a large extent unconscious, or appears as a sort of malaise, a dissatisfaction, for which people seek other motivations
>
> (pp. 135–136)

Here Freud introduces us to the idea of the guilt-substitute (Carveth, 2006, p. 179). From a psychoanalytic perspective, unconscious guilt may take the form of a wide range of such substitutes: anxiety states, hysterical and psychosomatic symptoms, depression, masochism, patterns of self-defeat and self-harm, and so on – conditions that, on the surface, often appear to have nothing whatever to do with issues of morality and guilt (Carveth & Carveth, 2003).

Freud taught us that unconscious guilt is often expressed in guilt-substitutes, painful symptoms of many types, and patterns of self-torment and self-sabotage operating in people's lives without any accompanying consciousness of guilt. But by equating guilt and the need for punishment, Freud missed the opportunity to discriminate between the two fundamentally different types of guilt that were subsequently distinguished by the psychoanalyst Melanie Klein (1948) and her followers: namely, persecutory guilt on the one hand, and depressive or reparative guilt on the other (Grinberg, 1964). If I injure someone and while he bleeds I self-flagellate, that is useless persecutory guilt, but if I put down my cat-o'-nine-tails and get my first-aid kit and begin bandaging, that is reparative guilt. Both primitive (persecutory) and mature (reparative) guilt may be rendered unconscious through defensive processes such as repression, projection, etc.

It is commonly thought that guilt is a useless and harmful emotion that we should get rid of. But that applies only to persecutory guilt, which is utterly narcissistic, self-involved, and irrelevant to the needs of the injured party. In reparative guilt we manage to get our minds off ourselves long enough to take note of the needs of the injured other and to make reparation.

Like grandiose self-worship, persecutory guilt and shame are narcissistic states, only focused upon the defects and inadequacies rather than the superiority of the self. In their narcissistic self-obsession they are asocial, even at times antisocial states. In contrast, reparative guilt is prosocial; it entails what Klein (1946) called depressive anxiety (which is not to be confused with depression) or what Winnicott (1965) refers to as the capacity for concern for the other.

Because he did not distinguish the two types of guilt, persecutory and reparative, when Freud (1930) regretted the growing burden of guilt imposed on humanity by civilization (owing to the need to preserve social order through inhibition of antisocial drives), he had only persecutory guilt in mind. Consequently, he was unable to see that while society certainly needs less persecutory guilt, it needs much more reparative guilt.

Beyond this, the failure to distinguish the two types of guilt prevented Freud from recognizing how persecutory guilt (self-punishment) often serves as a defence against or an evasion of the depressive guilt leading to reparation. People often seem to prefer to indulge for years in orgies of self-punishment (brought about in a myriad of subtle and not-so-subtle ways) rather than consciously own up to their faults, wrongdoings, sins, and crimes; confess; and repent through genuine contrition and reparation.

As much psychopathology is grounded in unconscious guilt and self-punishment, the path of contrition is the way to mental and spiritual health. Although over a century and a half ago, this was understood by Kierkegaard (1849), it is still a truth rejected by mainstream psychiatry, psychology, and psychoanalysis, which have been and still are committed to the de-moralization and medicalization of emotional disturbance. Though many of those who recognized the root of mental suffering in sin were, like Kierkegaard, religious, there is no need for religion in order to re-moralize mental suffering by understanding and coming to grips psychotherapeutically with its origins in guilt. For today it is widely understood that ethics require no religious foundation. We do not need God in order to know right from wrong, as recent research on other primate species (De Waal, 1997) and very young children (Bloom, 2010, 2013) makes clear. Whereas the superego is internalized from the culture, the conscience is founded in nature.

At the heart of much emotional suffering is guilt stemming not merely from wrongful acts but also from antisocial wishes, phantasies, and emotions of hate, envy, greed, and lust. When repressed, such guilt generates the torments of the damned. When it becomes conscious it can be worked through in such a way that, through repentance and reparation, mental peace and well-being may ultimately be restored. The self-punishment resulting from refusal to acknowledge guilt may be no more consciously recognized as such than its grounds.

In addition to the distinctions between persecutory and reparative, and conscious and unconscious guilt, other varieties may be distinguished. Since value judgment lies outside the means-end calculations that are the province of rationality, one cannot properly speak of rational or irrational moral judgment or guilt. Hence, we need instead to distinguish guilt that is justified or valid from the standpoint of mature conscience from guilt inflicted by the superego that may not be justified at all in this sense.

Only by being brought to consciousness can guilt be critically evaluated and found to be justified or unjustified. A patient for years unconsciously punished herself for her sister's death. On becoming conscious of this she realized she was not responsible for the death, but only for wishing it and being both gratified and devastated by it. Therapeutic reality-testing can be applied to guilt when it becomes conscious. Some guilt is entirely justified, some is not.

Freud (1923) argued that some guilt is not properly one's own, but is "borrowed" from another (p. 50, fn.) who, as Fernando (2000) explains, is usually a narcissistic parent who contrives to have a child carry the burden of guilt the parent refuses to bear. In reality, such guilt is not borrowed but induced through the unconscious process of interpersonal projective identification – Wilfred Bion's (1962) extension of Melanie Klein's (1946) original concept. It is not as if the child asked to borrow the guilt, nor does the parent want it back. There is a kind of victim-blaming in the idea of "borrowed" guilt, just as there was in Freud's (1896) calling what was really a theory of child abuse a "seduction theory."

Nietzsche (1887) taught us about guilt-induction. In direct battle with the strong, the weak will lose, but if they create an ethic in which strength is evil ("the meek shall inherit the earth") and get their oppressors to believe it, they (the strong) will fall on their own swords. The "will to power of the weak" is expressed through guilt-induction.

Beyond attempting to induce guilt in those who are envied, they may be directly targeted by those "marching under the banner of the superego" who have what Racker (1957) called a "mania for reproaching" (p. 141). In the face of a morally righteous attack, the victim's archaic superego and primitive guilt is awakened and undermines rational ego-functioning, the capacity to think, and the courage to conscientiously stand up for core values in the face of the mob.

Some guilt is entirely defensive: the unloved child protects against recognizing the parental failure to love by seeing itself as unlovable – Fairbairn's (1952) "moral defence."

Survival guilt is related to the guilt that Freud (1916) recognized is often associated with success and leads to its fear or to being wrecked by it. If I survive (or succeed), I feel, more or less unconsciously, that my survival (or success) is a crime against those who died (or failed), simply because a part of me is glad it was them and not me who died (or failed), or perhaps I had harboured death wishes (or failure wishes) toward them, or perhaps to survive (or succeed) I did things I'm not proud of.

Kierkegaard (1849) drew our attention to an unavoidable type of existential guilt: if I fail to actualize my potentials and grow as a human being I fail myself, but if I change and develop I may grow "beyond" others to whom I am attached and I may even have to leave them behind. Because my duties toward myself and toward others may conflict, I may find myself faced with a catch-22 in which I incur guilt no matter what I do.

Karl Jaspers (1947), among others, taught us about collective guilt. Above and beyond the guilt due to our personal wrongdoings and failures of responsibility is that arising from the misdeeds of our communities and nations. I believe that we in the West suffer from a kind of free-floating guilt, more or less unconscious, that we tend to attribute to our failings as individuals, but that may also arise from the fact that our relative affluence rests on the unconscionable exploitation of the poor, both at home and abroad. In recent years such free-floating guilt arises in the face of anthropogenic climate disruption and from growing recognition of the damage we have and are inflicting upon Mother Earth.

Chapter 2

Conscience

Most dictionaries define conscience as an inner faculty or voice that distinguishes right from wrong and generates guilt when we choose the latter. Prior to widespread secularization in the West, conscience was considered a manifestation of the divine, the *Vox Dei*, in an otherwise "fallen" human nature. Moral conflict was depicted as a battle between the divine and the demonic, between Christ and Old Adam, with conscience pulling toward the former and away from the latter.

With the Enlightenment and the rise of secular social science, conscience came to be seen as a social product, a manifestation in the individual psyche of social norms (folkways, mores, and laws) internalized in socialization. Now individual moral conflict was associated with tensions among the different elements of the psyche, much as Plato (380 BCE) had conceived it as conflict among the three elements of the soul – Appetite, Reason, and Spirit.

In "The Ego and the Id," Freud (1923) adapted Plato's (380 BCE) model, renaming appetite *Id*, reason *Ego*, and spirit *Superego*. At the same time, regrettably, he chose to make conscience a superego function, viewing it as a representative of the culture formed through the child's internalization of the parental superegos. Moral conflict now entailed either intersystemic conflict among superego, ego, and id, or intrasystemic conflict within the superego between incompatible internalized norms deriving from socialization into conflicting cultures, subcultures, or incompatible parental value-systems, as in so-called "schismatic" families (Lidz et al., 1965).

DOI: 10.4324/9781003347514-2

In identifying conscience with the superego, Freud made it a social product, an embodiment of the normative, rather than a moral force capable of conflicting with and morally challenging the social norms. Just as in relativistic social science a society could only be judged immoral from the standpoint of another society's equally relative morality, for psychoanalysis the superego could only be judged immoral by another superego representing the conflicting values of a different culture or subculture. Conflict between internalized norms and some other, non-internalized source of conscience – between a societal voice and a voice that in some manner transcends the merely societal and is capable of judging it – became difficult to posit in a purely secular context, a world without God, although adherents of various forms of humanism attempted to do so by positing universal human rights and needs (Fromm, 1947). C.G. Jung (1958) is exceptional in this respect for he clearly grasped the distinction between the merely culturally derived superego and a conscience that he saw as archetypal and grounded in nature.

As both a sociologist of religion and a religious sociologist, Peter Berger (1965) was able to transcend the dominant social science discourse in this respect, pointing out how belief in a "sacred cosmos" representing the laws of God reveals the merely human, socially constructed and, hence, relative nature of the "nomos" or normative order. For Hegel (1807) Sophocles' *Antigone* embodies the conflict between societal law, King Creon's refusal to bury an enemy of the state, and an ethic grounded in something more fundamental, a profound sense of what we owe to those with whom we are in relationship, as in Antigone's conscience-driven obligation to bury her brother.

While the idea of an ethic grounded in something more fundamental than the socially constructed laws of men has usually been associated with the sacred laws of God, today a purely secular social science and psychoanalysis can conceive this voice in entirely non-religious, non-supernatural terms, as emanating from the innate, unlearned attachment systems (Bowlby, 1969–1980) we share with our primate cousins. We are social by nature, not through the imposition of sociality upon an allegedly asocial or antisocial nature. We come into the world programmed to attach to the primary caretakers upon whose nurturance we depend for survival and development and with whom we form early identifications. Recent animal research (De Waal, 1997) has demonstrated the biological roots of conscience in humans and other primates, and recent infant research (Bloom, 2013) has shown a preference for right (helpful) over wrong (harmful) in infants as young as three months of age. Beyond the biological foundation of conscience are the infant's early identifications with nurturers: if they have survived, infants know what it is to receive love and feel the need to return it.

But even the most attuned and responsive caretakers cannot entirely protect infants and children from inevitable frustrations. Given their cognitive immaturity, they will inevitably experience their primary caretakers as both gratifying and depriving, both nurturing and persecuting. For Melanie Klein (1952) and Wilfred Bion (1962), the absent good breast is experienced as a present bad attacking breast. Hence, children will identify with both the nurturer and the aggressor. In my view (Carveth 2013, 2015, 2016), the former forms the core of conscience (the origin of what Grinberg [1964] distinguishes as reparative guilt), while the latter forms the core of the superego (the origin of punitive or persecutory guilt) to which later cultural internalizations are added.

Freud's (1923) collapsing of the distinction between superego and conscience made it difficult for us to conceive of, let alone study, conflicts between them. For example, a good deal of the PTSD seen in returning soldiers involves the "moral injury" (Nash, 2012) suffered by those who, in obedience to parental and military authority (superego), committed unconscionable acts for which they are unable to forgive themselves. As we will see in the next chapter, Sagan (1988) utilizes Mark Twain's (1885) *The Adventures of Huckleberry Finn* to illustrate the conflict.

Sometimes the cultural norms internalized into the superego may be congruent with the conscience formed through attachment and experiences of loving care on the part of nurturers with whom we identify. Sometimes, in addition to teaching us how to channel our hate toward scapegoats (Girard, 1989) of various sorts, a society may teach us to return love for love received. But giving love because we have been taught we ought to love is not at all the same thing as loving out of an intrinsic tendency and need to love.

I think it is quite evident we do not need God to be good; we need only be able to hear the voice of conscience, though some people have ironclad defences against this. People who do hear and seek to follow their conscience often find themselves in conflict with their society and the superego embodying its commands. Often, they feel called to conscientiously object and sometimes to defy their superegos and their societies in the name of conscience. Abraham felt called by God to sacrifice Isaac. How could he be sure the voice he heard was God's, or that he was the Abraham being summoned? While Kierkegaard (1843) celebrates him as a "knight of faith" capable of "the religious suspension of the ethical," I would have preferred Abraham to have had enough conscience to engage in what I think of as "the ethical suspension of the religious" and, like Antigone, to defy the superego/authority masquerading as God in favour of attachment and love. Here the *Vox Dei* is revealed as nothing supernatural, but a manifestation of conscience and what Winnicott (1965) called our "going-on-being" or "true self."

Chapter 3

Guilt evasion in the self, society, and psychoanalysis

Despite my later analytic training, I have never been successful in setting aside my sociological imagination (Mills, 1959) and insulating sociological from psychological analysis and vice versa. In the last analysis, psychoanalysis, like every other element of the cultural/ideological superstructure, is shaped, I believe, though not entirely determined, by the socio-economic substructure.

For decades, what Freud (1933) himself regarded as "the preferred field of work for psychoanalysis," namely "the problems which the unconscious sense of guilt has opened up, its connections with morality, education, crime and delinquency" (p. 61), has been displaced in favour of a preoccupation with trauma, abuse, deprivation, and environmental failure, the ways we are "more sinned against than sinning" (*King Lear*, Act III, Scene 2).

Freud and his followers illuminated the ways in which we are often the unwitting agents of our suffering, unconsciously contriving to refined and perpetuate our childhood pain – clutching defeat from the jaws of victory; fearing success; being wrecked by success; committing crimes in order to be caught and punished (Freud, 1916); finding partners to punish us so we need not do it ourselves; developing addictions to destructive substances, activities, and people; developing painful hysterical and psychosomatic conditions – largely due to our unconscious guilt and the need for punishment for real or imagined sins or crimes.

But over time this perspective came increasingly to be superseded by a discourse of victimization at the hands of not-good-enough mothers; absent, authoritarian, or abusive fathers; and

DOI: 10.4324/9781003347514-3

other varieties of parental and societal failure. There is no denying the reality of trauma, exploitation, and injustice. But trauma
induces rage, mostly turned against the self. Although unjustified,
abused children nevertheless blame themselves and feel guilty
and ashamed.

Yet, according to Heinz Kohut (1977), "Guilty Man" had been
disappearing in our culture, being replaced by "Tragic Man," who
suffers not from internal conflicts among id (sexual and aggressive
drives), ego (reason and reality-testing), and superego (the harsh
inner judge), but from the emptiness and fragmentation states of
a disordered self.

Early on, Erik Erickson (1950, p. 279) wrote that whereas in the
past patients thought they knew who they were and who they ought
to be, but came to therapy because they were having trouble being
it, the modern patient doesn't know who he is or who he ought to
be. Two decades later, Herbert Marcuse (1970) claimed the Freudian conception of the structured and conflicted human psyche had
become obsolescent due to social changes producing the unstruc-
tured personality that Christopher Lasch (1979) referred to as "the
narcissistic personality of our time."

Of course, decades earlier, all this had been prefigured in the
literature of existentialism and the "theatre of the absurd" (Esslin,
1961) – perhaps most clearly in Albert Camus' (1942) novel
L'Etranger. When his mother dies, or he is having sex with a
woman who wants him to say he loves her, or he shoots a stran-
ger on the beach, or a priest offers to hear his confession prior to
his execution – Meursault feels nothing and remains indifferent.
Many contemporary psychoanalysts seem no longer able to see or
hear, let alone speak, to the unconscious guilt lurking behind and
driving this behaviour. However empty, bored and indifferent he
is, Meursault manages both to kill and get himself killed.

By the late 1950s, Sandler (1960) had already noticed that in
the indexing of cases at the Hampstead Clinic there was a "tendency to veer away from the conceptualization of material in
superego terms"; he was wondering why "therapists have preferred to sort their clinical material in terms of object relation-
ships, ego activities, and the transference, rather than in terms
of the participation of the superego" (p. 129). Two decades later,

Arlow (1982) observed, "Superego function has been shunted to one side by the current preoccupation with the persistence of the regressive reactivation of archaic idealizations" (p. 230) and that "the concept superego itself rarely appears as the central topic of a clinical or theoretical contribution" (p. 229).

Wurmser (1998) referred to the superego as the "sleeping giant" of contemporary psychoanalysis. While the giant slept, having been anaesthetized in both society at large and the psychoanalytic thinking it encouraged, the foundations were laid for the dismantlement of the social state and the economic crisis of 2007–2008. The flight from self-regulation (superego, guilt, and conscience) in psychoanalysis paralleled deregulation in the economy and society.

It was no accident that the forgetting or evasion of guilt in psychoanalytic thought coincided with the shift from productive industrial to consumer capitalism, the emergence of the "culture of narcissism," and the rise of neoliberalism or market fundamentalism. Ironically, the psychoanalytic preoccupation in the 1970s and 1980s with the states of shame suffered by narcissistic characters incapable of bearing depressive or reparative guilt coincided with the flight from guilt in psychoanalysis itself.

While shame is a manifestation of the self-preoccupation that characterizes the culture of narcissism, depressive or reparative (as distinct from persecutory) guilt is not, for mature guilt involves moving beyond the realm of self-obsession (the paranoid-schizoid position) into the field of recognition and concern for the other (the depressive or reparative position). In several streams of psychoanalytic thought the central role of guilt-evasion in pathological narcissism was obscured – an instance of what Russell Jacoby (1975) referred to as the "social amnesia" in which "society remembers less and less faster and faster" and in which "the sign of the times is thought that has succumbed to fashion" (p. 1).

Prior to the 1960s, psychoanalysts viewed superego analysis as central to the analytic process. Some analysts never lost sight of Freudian and Kleinian insight into the dynamics of guilt and self-punishment – in what Freud (1916) called "moral masochism," the varied patterns of self-harm and self-defeat. In *Man Against*

Himself, Karl Menninger (1938) documented the range of "guilt substitutes" and "suicide equivalents" through which we unconsciously torture ourselves and unknowingly practice what I view as a type of archaic sacrificial religion. Just as an animal caught in a trap may chew off its leg to survive, so we placate that the savage god Freud and his followers called the superego, seeking to escape with our lives by sacrificing our careers, our marriages, our health.

Many of the newer psychoanalytic approaches that came to prominence in the 1970s and 1980s downplayed intra-psychic conflict and guilt in favour of an emphasis upon trauma, deprivation, abuse, and neglect by caretakers. In my view, what was lost sight of by adherents of these newer perspectives is the fact that trauma, abuse, deprivation, and neglect generate rage, most of which gets turned away from the caretakers and back upon the self, resulting in its manifest fragmentation and emptiness. If we find a crater, we might suspect a bomb. Several classic Westerns open upon a scene of death and devastation: the wagon-train overturned and on fire, one slowly turning wheel festooned with arrows. We see the result of an attack, but not the violence itself.

Rather than emptiness directly reflecting inadequate provision, it is generally a result of reactive aggression fuelling what Bion (1959, p. 313) called "the ego-destructive superego." It is for this reason that a simple therapy through provision of what Kohut referred to as "selfobject function" and Bacal (1985) called "optimal responsiveness" is, although a necessary element of therapeutic technique, ultimately insufficient because it fails to address the key pathogen: the ego-destructive superego that generates the range of persecutory states that characterize the disordered self.

But not all of the guilt from which we suffer is our own: some is, in Freud's (1923, p. 50, fn.) unfortunate and misleading term, "borrowed" from others who, as Fernando (2000) explains, induce in others the guilt they themselves find unbearable. But here we encounter the kind of victim-blaming we saw in Freud's calling his observations on the sexual abuse of children a "seduction" theory. In the present case, the child did not ask to "borrow" the guilt that was induced, nor does the parent want it back!

Here we see that, in addition to the patterns of self-damage Freud called "moral masochism" that entail the deployment of reactive rage against the self, there is the "immoral sadism" in which such rage is discharged against others – scapegoats – who are substituted for the self as the target of the sadistic superego. In order to escape its attacks, some people join it, "identify with the aggressor" (Anna Freud, 1936), and inflict punishment as a way of avoiding it – like those death-camp prisoners, the "Kapos," who became the assistants of the guards, or like hostages who identify with and join their captors as in so-called "Stockholm syndrome." In these ways a critical superego is embraced and self-persecution is escaped by targeting others.

Today, some so-called "social justice warriors" display what Heinrich Racker (1957) called "a mania for reproaching" (p. 141). If one marches "under the banner of the superego," focusing attention on the abusers and identifying with victims ("Me Too!"), one's own immorality may for a time be obscured – until, that is, someone finds the courage to accuse the accusers. In this connection it is well to recall that memorable moment when Joe McCarthy's superegoic attacks were called out as unconscionable by Joseph Welch: "Let us not assassinate this lad further, Senator. You have done enough. Have you no sense of decency?" (U.S. Senate Archive, June 9, 1954).

There is no need to call into question descriptions of manifest social changes in the presenting problems patients bring to therapists, other than to say the generalizations are exaggerated. Just as we continue to see the old hysterias (tics, paralyses, globus hystericus, etc.) that some claimed had disappeared being replaced by the "new hysterias" (fibromyalgia, chronic fatigue, environmental illness, irritable bowel syndrome, etc.), so we see plenty of the manifestly guilty variety in addition to emptiness depression.

For the psychoanalyst, as for the courtroom judge, a person's claim that he is not guilty, or does not feel guilty is the beginning, not the end, of an inquiry. Evidence must be marshalled and critically reviewed. In fact, it is my thesis that Tragic Man and Guilty Man are not distinctly different disorders at all, for progress in therapy generally reveals that underneath the manifest emptiness of the former lies the self-directed aggression of the latter. I can well imagine having

Camus' Meursault on my analytic couch and witnessing the gradual emergence of the rage, and then the shame, and then the guilt, and then the tears underlying his manifest indifference. Meursault is a frozen man in need of therapeutic thawing.

The emptiness and fragmentation of the self is brought about precisely by the persecutory and annihilating superego. Of course, this is not merely the Freudian superego formed at the end of the Oedipal phase at five or six years of age, but the pregenital superego formed in the first year of life as an internalization of the bad, persecutory breast, as Melanie Klein (1946) taught us – an annihilating part-object that lies beneath and at the core of the later Oedipal development.

Over the last decade or so in psychoanalysis, issues concerning the superego, guilt, and conscience have to some extent at least returned from repression. Around the time of the Occupy movement and the emergence of whistle-blowers such as Assange, Manning, and Snowden, psychoanalytic books and articles began to appear with titles such as *You Ought To! A Psychoanalytic Study of the Superego and Conscience* (Barnett, 2007); *Guilt and Its Vicissitudes: Psychoanalytic Reflections on Morality* (Hughes, 2008); *The Quest for Conscience and the Birth of the Mind* (Reiner, 2009); *The Still Small Voice: Psychoanalytic Reflections on Guilt and Conscience* (Carveth, 2013); "Reflections on the Absence of Morality in Psychoanalytic Theory and Practice" (Frattaroli, 2013); and *Guilt: Origins, Manifestations, and Management* (Akhtar, Ed., 2013).

No doubt this partial "comeback" was a reflection in psychoanalysis of a dawning recognition that the culture of narcissism had gotten us into hot water. What Rangell (1980) had described in *The Mind of Watergate* as the "syndrome of the compromise of integrity" led eventually to the 2008 crisis of "casino capitalism." In conflict among ego, id, and superego, defences may be directed against the id, as in neurosis, but also against the ego, the superego, and the conscience – that is, against the regulatory functions of the mind – leading to those forms of psychic deregulation we call narcissistic and, in extreme, psychopathic (Carveth, 2007). In the wider society the neoliberal passion for deregulation advocated by the likes of Ayn Rand and pushed by Thatcher, Reagan, Milton Freedman, Alan

Greenspan, and a host of others laid the basis for the emergence of the demoralized, "post-truth" world of Donald Trump.

Although generally found on opposite sides of the political spectrum, today the narcissistic/sociopathic types on the right are joined on the (pseudo) left by the normopaths (McDougall, 1993; Bollas, 2017) who reproach, condemn, and seek to cancel (i.e., destroy) those they judge immoral, politically incorrect, or otherwise "beyond the pale."

Currently we witness pathology involving both the inhibition and the hypertrophy of the superego: people who evade guilt either by floating morality (the syndrome of the compromise of integrity) or by moralistically identifying with the superego and attacking others, their scapegoats. The latter strategy may be seen on the pseudo-left, but also on the right, on the part of righteous conservatives who seem to take for granted their divine right to rule. They often manage to induce in any opponents the feeling that they are being naughty children. Those identified with authority often succeed in crippling any opposition by evoking in opponents, through projective identification, the archaic, inhibiting superego.

Today, conscientious whistle-blowers who are persecuted by the establishment, such as Snowden and Assange, are joined by those – left, right and centre – who oppose the "cancel culture" promoted by the new authoritarians, aided and abetted by "woke" centrists willing to suppress any qualms in favour of a "moral" consensus. In the face of organized protests by groups who cannot bear the exercise of free speech, people are targeted and oppressed while "liberal" authorities, who should know better, cave in the face of pressure from fascism "marching under the banner of the superego."

Psychoanalysis originally opposed repression and censorship. It sought to make the unconscious conscious and to emancipate people through "free speech" and "free association" and from inhibitions, symptoms and anxiety, putting everything into words. It suspended moral judgment in order to bring socially unacceptable elements of the soul, infantile and polymorphous perverse sexuality and aggression, into the light. While we have rightfully sought to overcome our racism, sexism, heterosexism, classism, and other socially structured patterns of injustice, today, in the face of a new puritanism, it might well be difficult, even impossible in some psychoanalytic circles to teach Freud on sexuality, let alone Robert Stoller (1975, 1979, 1985) and Otto Kernberg (1991, 1993) who argue sexuality has to be, to a degree, transgressive (i.e., naughty) in order to be worth having.

Today, as always, human beings suffer conflict among id, ego, superego, and conscience and resort to defensive strategies in attempts to minimize frustration, anxiety, and guilt. In addition to the defences and resistances inhibiting the sexual and aggressive drives of the id, there are those directed against both superego and conscience, resulting in the syndromes of compromised integrity. One variant of these is that in which identification with the aggressor (the hypercritical superego) defends against both the id (which is projected onto the offenders) and the conscience, resulting in unconscionable sadistic attacks upon those whose speech or actions are considered to be incorrect and reprehensible. This is an increasingly widespread social pathology that is spreading like a virus, especially in the humanities and social science faculties of North American universities, with the contagion spreading even into psychoanalytic societies.

Unfortunately, Freud's blurring of the distinction between superego and conscience has impaired psychoanalysts' capacity to recognize and avoid infection by this form of psychopathology. In this area psychoanalysis is as vulnerable as the general public to abusive behaviour enacted "under the banner of the superego" by police, judges, priests, and social justice warriors. Psychoanalysts should, of all people, remember that "you can't tell a book by its cover." Beneath what appears to be an admirable concern for justice may lie, as Nietzsche (1887) among others taught us, a destructive will to power and revenge driven by envy, resentment, and other forms of malice that need to be called out and opposed by people of conscience.

In my view, unconscious guilt and the unconscious need for punishment motivates myriad forms of self-sabotage and self-destructiveness in people whose chosen guilt-substitutes allow them to have no clue that they suffer from guilt. As Freud (1923, pp. 49–50) put it:

> In the end we come to see that we are dealing with what may be called a "moral" factor . . . which is finding its satisfaction in the illness and refuses to give up the punishment of suffering. . . . But as far as the patient is concerned this sense of guilt is dumb; it does not tell him he is guilty; he does not feel guilty, he feels ill.

Both "Tragic Man" and the new authoritarians are unaware of their guilt, in the one case through its repression, in the other through its projection. There are many ways to define the goal of clinical psychoanalysis, but developing a conscience capable of both bearing mature guilt and standing up to the sadistic superego, neither embracing nor capitulating to it, should be added to our list.

Chapter 4

Conscience vs. superego

Since, according to Freud (1940), the superego "represents more than anything the cultural past" (p. 205), we have tended to conceptualize inner moral conflict either as between internalized values and incompatible, generally antisocial, sexual, and aggressive impulses arising from the id, or as incompatible internalized value-orientations (between, say, the values of the old country and those of the new). We have not viewed inner moral conflict as between superego and conscience, the latter being conceived either as a separate mental structure or as prosocial impulses (grounded in attachment) arising from the id.

In practical terms, the Freudian tradition has mostly conceived the id as antisocial, despite grounding *Eros* (the life drive) as well as *Thanatos* (the so-called death drive) there. When the libidinal aspect of the id has been considered, it has mostly been in regard to transgressive, incestuous, or antisocial libidinal impulses, not its prosocial, communal, and loving manifestations. Instead of turning away from the idea of a conscience capable of conflicting with the socially derived superego, as Freud (1923) did in "The Ego and the Id," the Freudians might have grounded conscience in the prosocial id, in those manifestations of libido (*Eros*) that are the basis of attachment and love. In a broad sense and within a different conceptual frame, this is what Carl Gustav Jung (1958) did in his insightful paper, "A Psychological View of Conscience." Here he clearly distinguished societal values, socially constructed and internalized norms, from both the *Vox Dei* and a conscience grounded in the natural (the archetypal) as distinct from the

DOI: 10.4324/9781003347514-4

socially acquired. But Freud was so caught up in the outmoded 19th-century "myth of the beast" that he generally conceived our animal nature as "beastly," failing to appreciate the cooperative, prosocial dimensions of animality and projecting morality onto the often immoral and moralistic superego.

We have not been blind to the fact that sometimes what we have been taught does not correspond with what we feel or desire, but we have focused on situations in which what we have been taught is moral while what we feel or desire is immoral or antisocial. We have mostly ignored situations in which what we have been taught is immoral while what we feel or desire is moral, composed of *prosocial* feelings derived from our mammalian and primate heritage, our attachments and libidinal object relations.

In his classic study, *Freud, Women and Morality: The Psychology of Good and Evil*, Eli Sagan (1988) cites Mark Twain's (1885/2005, ch. 31) depiction of "Huck's Dilemma" to illuminate our bias: while the racist superego Huck has internalized from his culture demands that he turn his runaway slave companion, Jim, in to the authorities, his conscience requires him to protect the friend he loves. After an agonizing mental struggle, Huck finally decides conscientiously to defy his superego and tears up the letter informing on his friend:

> But somehow I couldn't seem to strike no places to harden me against him, but only the other kind. . . . I was a-trembling, because I'd got to decide, forever, betwixt two things, and I knowed it. I studied a minute, sort of holding my breath, and then says to myself: "All right, then, i'll go to hell" – and tore it up.

Huck's conflict is between an immoral moral imperative internalized from a racist society and a sense of obligation derived from feelings of attachment and love.

In *Les Misérables* (vol. 5, bk. 4, "Javert Derailed"), Victor Hugo (1862) offers a moving illustration of the conflict between superego and conscience. The policeman/superego, Javert, comes finally to be touched by conscience, discovering "that one cherishes beneath one's breast of bronze something absurd and disobedient which almost resembles a heart!" As a result,

> A whole new world was dawning on his soul: kindness accepted and repaid, devotion, mercy, indulgence, violences committed by pity on austerity, respect for persons, no more definitive condemnation, no more conviction, the possibility of a tear in the eye of the law.

Confronted with the "terrible rising of an unknown moral sun," Javert, who until now has been entirely identified with the superego, chooses suicide.

While internal moral conflict can involve incompatible internalized values (e.g., sometimes it is unkind to tell the truth), and while internalized moral values may certainly conflict with antisocial id impulses, sometimes internalizations conflict with prosocial feelings and impulses deriving from libidinal attachments. And sometimes we have conflicting attachments. But what I want to emphasize is that in our thinking about conflict between superego and id, we have had mostly the antisocial (incestuous and aggressive) id and mostly the prosocial superego in mind, neglecting both the antisocial superego and the prosocial id.

Note that Huck's dilemma does not involve an abnormal, pathological, or archaic superego but a normal, albeit a racist, one. Until fairly recently a homophobic, heterosexist superego was normative in psychoanalytic circles and for years "under the banner of the superego" we rejected gay applicants for training. Many of us now think that superego was immoral. Although we have understood the superego as both aggression turned back against the self and values internalized from parents and society, we have devoted little attention to the racism, sexism, heterosexism, classism, childism (Young-Bruehl, 2012), possessive individualism, commodity fetishism, etc. that characterize the normal, unconscionable superego. Where we have seen the immorality and destructiveness of the superego at all, we have attributed it to an "abnormal" or "pathological" superego, or to "superego lacunae," thus resisting recognizing that the superego is very often, to varying degrees, pathologically normal, that is, a "normopathic" (McDougall, 1993) or "normotic" (Bollas, 1989) phenomenon.

Despite Freud's awareness of the role of the sadistic super-ego in psychopathology and his overall view of it as a hostile and destructive inner force that at times may even amount to "a pure culture of the death instinct" (Freud, 1923, p. 52) and despite his resultant call for its clinical "demolition" (Freud, 1940, p. 180), in his sociological writings he contradictorily represented it as a *prosocial* force saving civilization from the antisocial forces of the "beastly" id. Freud saw the drives as arising from a somatic source, from the animal aspect of our nature. While transcending common sense in many respects, here Freud succumbed to it, projecting our uniquely human destructiveness onto the beasts and the animal in humankind, when animals are seldom beastly, at least not in the ways humans often are (Carveth, 2012).

Thanks to the work of Robert J. Lifton (1986) on *The Nazi Doctors*, whom he shows were not for the most part psychopaths but superego-driven, racist ideologues, and similar studies of terrorism, "soul-murder" (Shengold, 1989), and other forms of human destructiveness, we are finally forced to recognize the roots of human evil in the superego and the ego, not merely or even primarily in the id. Those responsible for the death camps, like those responsible for dropping atom bombs on civilian populations, were not for the most part psychopathic demons but superego-driven "do-gooders" who employed sophisticated ego function in the service of destruction. In tending to think of conflict as between a moral superego and an immoral id, we have overlooked both the immorality of the superego and the morality of the id.

We have suffered from a similarly contradictory attitude toward guilt, sometimes seeing it as sadism turned against the self and at others as a sign of advancement toward a more mature level of psychic development (Ury, 1998). This contradiction was finally resolved when Klein and her co-workers (Grinberg, 1964) differentiated *persecutory* guilt (including shame) from *depressive* or *reparative* guilt, Winnicott's (1963/1965a) "capacity for concern" for the other. In this light we are finally able to see that while in civilization we need less of the former (persecutory guilt – superego), we need much more of the latter (reparative guilt – conscience).

Because he failed to distinguish these two fundamentally different types of guilt, Freud also failed to grasp the role of persecutory guilt (superego) as a *defence* against and a *resistance* to reparative guilt (conscience) – that is, the role of the superego in guilt-evasion. People often prefer orgies of self-punishment to acknowledging wrongdoing, bearing depressive guilt or concern, and forgoing both narcissism and masochism in favour of contrition and conscientious, reparative activity. In this connection it is notable that we have come to associate narcissism as such with its grandiose form, overlooking the negative narcissism of the self-disparaging but no less self-obsessed depressive who may carry on attacking himself forever as a resistance to facing his guilt.

Following that side of Freud's (1940) clinical thinking that called for "the slow demolition of the hostile superego" (p. 180), Ferenczi (1927/1928) wrote, "Only a complete dissolution of the super-ego can bring about a radical cure" (p. 100). In this connection, Theodor Adorno (1966/1983) wrote, "A critique of the super-ego would have to turn into one of the society that produces the superego; if psychoanalysts stand mute here, they accommodate the ruling norm" (p. 274). Unlike Ferenczi himself, who was both a political and a psychoanalytic radical, most psychoanalysts have pretty much stood mute here, accommodating the ruling norm.

Like Ferenczi, Franz Alexander (1925) regarded the superego as "an anachronism in the mind" (p. 25). The therapeutic task, he wrote, "is carried out by limiting the sphere of activity of the automatically-functioning super-ego, and transferring its role to the conscious ego" (p. 25). Because, following Freud (1923), most psychoanalysts have identified conscience with the super-ego, unlike Alexander, Ferenczi, and Freud himself, they have feared that demolition of the superego would be tantamount to the promotion of psychopathy. Hence they have called instead, like Strachey (1934), for its modification and maturation (Jacobson, 1964; Kernberg, 1976; Schafer, 1960; Gray, 1994; Britton, 2003) rather than its replacement by conscience. Freud, Alexander, and Ferenczi represent the minority view: against the immoral moralism of the superego they posit a conscience grounded in *thinking*, a rational ego function in which one thinks through the consequences of one's actions for oneself and others. We might formulate their dictum as "where superego was, there ego shall come to be."

But the problem with this, as with Freud's rationalism and his call for the dominance of the ego over superego and id, is that the rational ego is incapable of serving as a conscience. While thinking through the consequences of our actions for ourselves and others is *relevant* to moral decisions, reason cannot serve as an authority establishing one value over another. The knowledge that smoking causes cancer and that cancer can cause death is relevant to the decision of whether or not to smoke. But reason cannot establish that health is superior to illness or that life is worth living. More recently, Bion (1962) and, following him, Reiner (2009), found the basis for conscientious development beyond the rigid pseudo-moral superego in *thinking*. While the type of thinking they have in mind, involving "containment," reverie, alpha function, etc. and leading to "transformations in O," cannot be reduced to simple ratiocination, it remains significant that they choose to label the mental process they have in mind as "thinking."

In contrast to both Freudian and Bionian rationalism, Sagan (1988) recognized with Jean-Jacques Rousseau (1754) that conscience arises not from *reason* but from *feeling*, from what Rousseau called "pity" – sympathy or fellow-feeling. Our feelings of both sympathy and antipathy originate in our histories of attachment and object relations and in what Sagan viewed as our resulting identifications with the nurturer on one hand and with the aggressor on the other.

Given the fact/value disjunction, the confinement of reason and science to the *descriptive* field of the *is* and its incompetence with respect to the *prescriptive* field of the *ought*, as David Hume (1739–1740; 1748) taught us in the 18th century, we are forced to recognize that conscience is fundamentally grounded in non-rational, emotional processes of attachment, sympathy, concern, and love, not in the head but the heart – for, as Pascal (1669, p. 4) famously put it, "The heart has reasons reason cannot know." Even while recognizing the limits of reason, the later Freud placed his confidence in secondary-process thinking, regarding feeling, like primary process and the unconscious, with suspicion, associating it with madness rather than valuing it as a source of existential orientation, potential wisdom, and creativity. Due to this suspicion of feeling and overestimation of reason (which Sagan recognized as stemming from Freud's devaluation of the feminine, the pre-Oedipal, and the maternal) even those psychoanalysts who recognize the destructiveness of the superego have, for the most part, felt no need to posit a separate conscience, thinking that the ego itself can serve as a sufficient moral guide. For Freud (1933), "Our best hope for the future is that intellect – the scientific spirit, reason – may in process of time establish a dictatorship in the mental life of man" (p. 170). But anyone who, following Freud's recommendation, actually succeeded in establishing a "dictatorship of the intellect," achieving dominance of the ego over id and superego, and living as an "enlightened hedonist" in accordance with the pleasure and reality principles would today be rightly diagnosed as a pathological narcissist or a psychopath. Freud (1914) himself, it will be recalled, wrote,

> A strong egoism is a protection against falling ill, but in the last resort we must begin to love in order not to fall ill, and we are bound to fall ill if, in consequence of frustration, we are unable to love.
>
> (p. 84)

Conscience is grounded in attachment and love and is beyond both the pleasure and reality principles, as well as being beyond the narcissism in which, as Freud (1914) pointed out, the other we "love" is really nothing more than the self we are, or were, or wish to be.

While few psychoanalysts have followed Freud, Alexander, and Ferenczi and defined the goal of psychoanalysis as *demolition* of the superego, most have shared Strachey's implicit devaluation of the harsh superego and his conception of the analytic cure as involving, among other things, substantial superego modification or modulation, a development conceived most often as advance beyond an archaic or pathological superego toward a more mature or healthy one. The use of terms such as "archaic" versus "mature," and "pathological" versus "healthy," cloaks what is really a moral judgment defining love and forgiveness as superior to hate and retribution. Psychoanalysts have traditionally attempted to "demoralize" psychoanalytic discourse in this way, representing it as an ethically neutral, "value-free," scientific, and medical discipline when, as I have argued (Carveth, 2013, ch. 1), it is and always has been a thoroughly moral enterprise from beginning to end. At least in Freud's own writings the demoralizing disguise at times wore very thin, as in his demand (Freud, 1914) that we overcome narcissism in favour of object love and his hope, expressed at the end of "Civilization and Its Discontents," that "the other of the two 'Heavenly Powers' . . . , eternal *Eros*, will make an effort to assert himself in the struggle with his equally immortal adversary" (Freud, 1930, p. 144). To those who would inflate the notion of analytic neutrality to condemn as unanalytic the making of such value judgments, I would point out that our very showing up to analyze – that is, our rejection of suicide and our choice of life over death – is an implicit endorsement of a value judgment enacted in every session.

But while some psychoanalysts accepted Freud's view of the superego's sadism and therefore sought to either radically modify it (Strachey) or demolish it altogether as a bad internal persecutory object (Freud, Alexander, Ferenczi), Schafer (1960), reacting against Freud's own focus upon its sadism, advanced the idea of a "loving and beloved superego" that he cobbled together from small hints and suggestions appearing here and there in Freud's writings that Freud himself had notably not allowed to alter his overall view. Admitting that "Freud was not prepared to pursue to its end the line of thought leading to a loving and beloved superego or to integrate such a conception with his decisive treatment of the criticizing and feared superego" (Schafer, 1960, p. 163), Schafer nevertheless proceeded to do the job for him. Subsequent readers of Schafer's paper seem to have thought it revealed that Freud himself had a more benign view of the superego, when what the paper truly revealed was what Schafer and others wished had been his view, not the superego Freud actually gave us. I submit that Schafer's "loving and beloved superego" is not the superego at all, but the conscience.

In the work of Paul Gray (1994, ch. 5 and 6) one sees another retreat from Freud's predominant view of the superego, this time as one of the three structures of the mind, to a view of it as a defensive ego operation, which correctly emphasizes the role of retroflected aggression in superego formation while largely ignoring that of internalized cultural ideology. (Recall in this connection the quotation from Freud that opens this chapter.) Because it has represented itself as a cautious extension of Freudian insights, the degree to which post-Freudian ego psychology, including so-called modern conflict theory, represents a radical revision of Freudian theory and a retreat from some of its most radical insights has tended to escape recognition.

A sociologist might suggest that whereas Freud himself gave us a late-19th-century European father-superego, Schafer gave us that of mid-20th-century America. If this were so, it would imply social progress: getting a more modulated view of the superego because superegos had become modulated. But is that a fact or a wish? At the very time Schafer was advancing his view of the superego as more "Pop" than "*Vater*," Kohut (1978) was celebrating the passing of "Guilty Man" altogether in our culture.

Here we must boldly bring psychoanalytic thinking to bear and distinguish between what is conscious and what is unconscious. Perhaps as the result of changes in culture, gender roles, family structure, etc., harsh paternal authority had diminished and, at least on the conscious level, the authoritarian superego along with it. Yet Freud (1930, pp. 128–129) explained how a severe superego may result from a lenient upbringing, its severity having as much to do with the turning of aggression against the ego as with actual parental behaviour. Our clinical experience would suggest little decline in the role of the sadistic, tyrannical, unconscious superego in psychopathology. Of course, this is a point that one is in a position to affirm or deny only to the extent that in clinical work one still "listens with the third ear" (Reik, 1948) to the unconscious.

Schafer's post-Freudian revision of Freud's theory of the superego has, like Gray's (1994), been very influential, even among analysts not usually fond of revisionism, and for several reasons. First, it compensated to some extent for the lack of any concept of a loving and forgiving conscience with which to offset the harshness of the superego. And second, it did so without calling, like Alexander, Ferenczi, and Freud himself, for the superego's demolition. Even Britton (2003), who possesses a clear understanding of the role of the ego-destructive and envious superego in psychopathology, seeks only to reform it by liberating it from hostile, alien, internal, bad occupying forces rather than recognizing its core, as Klein and even Freud did (in his clinical writings at least), as a bad, persecutory, internal object. In calling for a strengthening of the ego and modification of the superego, Britton would certainly be joined by mainstream American psychoanalysis which, likewise, seeks only the "maturation" of the superego, rather than its subordination to conscience as the capacity for concern and reparation characteristic of depressive position functioning. The superego remains, after all, in unconscious phantasy, the parent, and out of our need to "honour thy mother and thy father" there remains strong resistance to anything approaching its radical critique. Can we liberate ourselves sufficiently from our parental complexes to be able to actually grow up and disempower the superego and subject it to the authority of conscience?

Psychoanalytic critique of the superego has focused almost exclusively upon its destructive manifestations in the life of the individual, in self-punishment, self-sabotage, masochism, depression, and suicide, not upon the morally objectionable internalized socio-cultural ideologies that the superego comprises and that are reflected even in its normative, let alone its pathological, expressions. Freud's (1923) incorporation of both conscience and ego-ideal into the superego hampers our capacity to undertake such a critique, for in the traditional view, the superego is the only judge and there is no other judge to judge it, no higher court of moral appeal. In this framework we can describe only superegos with different content, ones that are racist and sexist and ones that are less so, right-wing and left-wing ones, harsh and critical ones, or more loving and forgiving ones. But to move beyond description and to judge one superego as morally better or worse than another requires an autonomous basis for such moral judgment.

Whereas in the past social scientists and philosophers have often succumbed to the moral relativism arising from a view of morality as an entirely social product constructed in radically different ways in different historical and cultural contexts, today there exists widespread agreement regarding the existence of a universal moral standpoint beneath all cultural accretions and variations that holds simply that one ought not do to others what one does not wish to be done to oneself, the principle of reciprocity that Kant (1785) embodied in his categorical imperative. The universal moral norm of reciprocity constitutes the basis of both conscience and the conscientious critique of superego ideologies and practices that violate it. Without it, critics of the superego – such as Freud, Alexander, Ferenczi, Bion, and, more recently, Britton – have been forced to appeal to reason against the superego's moralism, a responsibility that, as we have seen, the rational ego is incapable of assuming.

While Freud recognized the role of *identification with the aggressor* in superego formation toward the end of the Oedipal phase, and Klein understood its role in formation of the pregenital superego (identification with the all-bad persecutory part-object), largely as the result of the essentially unrecognized work of Eli Sagan (1988) we have failed to grasp the pre-Oedipal roots of conscience in *identification with the nurturer*. If the superego comprises the aggressive drive (Freud's *Thanatos* or, preferably, Fromm's *necrophilic* impulse) turned on the self, and identification with the aggressor, then the conscience comprises the libidinal drive (or *Eros*, Fromm's *biophilia*) directed outward and inward, and identification with the nurturer. Whereas the superego derives from aggression, the conscience derives from libido, today understood to include a primary (unlearned) drive-based need for attachment. Whereas Freud (1920) advanced the bizarre idea of *Thanatos* as a biologically given, natural drive toward death, Fromm's (1964) *necrophilia* is an unnatural, pathological, and perverse turning away from life toward death due to frustration and trauma.

Even with the best caretaking imaginable, frustration is inevitable and generates hatred toward the primary object experienced as a persecutor. But, for Klein, "the newborn infant unconsciously feels that an object of unique goodness exists, from which a maximal gratification could be obtained and that this object is the mother's breast" (Klein et al., 1952, p.265). In primary love and attachment, together with the principle of reciprocity that takes the form not just of the talion law of hate for hate but also that of love for love, lie the drive foundations of conscience, the overlooked morality of the id mentioned above.

Value imperatives internalized from parents and society (superego) often generate something of a "false self" (Winnicott, 1960) on the basis of compliance that conflicts with desires arising from the "true self" and its need to express both its hatred toward the persecutory bad object – identification with which forms the core of the superego – and its love and gratitude toward the nurturing good object – identification with which forms the core of conscience and generates the need for prosocial behaviour and authentic self-expression.

One of the strengths of classical psychoanalysis has been its refusal to succumb to overly socialized, culturally determinist, entirely relational models of human nature, calling our attention to universal drives that conflict with social forces. While well aware of conflicts between social pressures and the drives of sex and aggression, we have paid little attention to those between social internalizations (superego) and moral feelings and obligations grounded in attachment and love (conscience). Conscience, grounded in *Eros*, frequently conflicts with superego, grounded in *Thanatos* (*necrophilia*). As Freud in his clinical writings understood, as distinct from his sociological speculations, and as Klein consistently grasped, the superego is, at its core, a bad, persecutory, internal object. What we have been calling the loving and beloved superego is the conscience. Therapeutic progress requires us to progressively erode the autonomy of the superego and bring it under the authority of and subject it to discipline by the conscience.

But instead of recognizing the superego as founded upon the bad object and calling for its subordination to conscience, we have preferred the idea of superego modification. In so doing we have failed to recognize that without conscience we lack any basis for judging one superego as superior to another. To reject the idea of conscience as separate from the superego and instead focus on the goal of superego maturation is self-contradictory, for we can distinguish a mature from an immature superego only by the standards of conscience.

There is no denying that the superego sometimes represents the internalization of cultural values congruent with conscience; in such cases one is pulled by both one's conscience and one's superego in prosocial directions, though even here the superego, as aggression retroflected against the self as well as internalized norms, will be more inclined to exhort and punish, while the conscience will push for change and reparation. In the following chapter, two case vignettes will be provided to illustrate these points.

Chapter 5

Two case vignettes

Case vignette 1: Mrs. A

Mrs. A, an ambitious young lawyer in her early thirties on the fast track to becoming a partner in a prestigious law firm, declined to take the full maternity leave to which she was entitled. This decision appeared to be grounded in her professional superego; her devotion to her profession, her firm, her colleagues, and her ideals of hard work; and also in her fear that to go on leave would cause her career to "stall in the water" as she had seen happen to other women colleagues whose careers never seemed to recover when they returned from "mat leave."

So, as soon as she was strong enough and her daughter stabilized on the bottle and attached to the live-in nanny, she had returned to work full time. Although her husband, an academic, helped to fill in, Mrs. A, though exhausted, was having trouble sleeping, being awakened by tormenting dreams and by the re-emergence of the migraine headaches that had troubled her for a time before her marriage but that had for a few years largely disappeared. In addition she was having occasional anxiety attacks that appeared to "come out of the blue" and for which she could find no conscious, rational reasons.

In her analytic psychotherapy it became evident that Mrs. A was feeling persecuted by a critical superego formed in identification with her "stay-at-home" mother and informed by her internalization from her family and the wider culture of ideals of maternalism from the standpoint of which she felt judged guilty

DOI: 10.4324/9781003347514-5

for "abandoning" her baby. Working through in these terms did not yield any significant relief, despite her attempts to reassure herself that her baby was being well taken care of and seemed to be doing well, as well as being reassured by her husband and others that she was spending "quality time" with her daughter, and so on.

It gradually became evident that, in addition to superego pressure, there were deeper sources of her guilt and self-punishment stemming from her deep love of and attachment to her child and her need to be with her to deliver the nurturance she longed to provide. Her final decision to take a leave of absence from the firm, despite whatever negative effects this might have on her career, did not appear to amount to a surrender to superego pressure, but rather to an act of conscience.

Mrs. A's professional and maternal ideals represented superego elements that pulled in opposite directions. Her conscience, though pulling in the same direction as her maternal superego, was grounded in her deep attachment to her child. Mrs. B's conflict was somewhat less complex.

Case vignette 2: Mrs. B

In her late teens and early twenties while in college, Mrs. B had had several brief but exciting homosexual affairs with girlfriends but by her senior year was dating men and had come to dismiss her earlier dalliances as meaningless. To her close girlfriends at that time she jokingly called herself a "LUG" (lesbian until graduation) or a "hasbian" (pronounced so as to rhyme with "lesbian"), a term defined by Urban Dictionary as "an adult female . . . who has affairs with women and declares herself lesbian when young but decides later that she's really hetero and becomes a totally straight *hausfrau*, married, PTA, making apple pies, the works."

During her last year of college, Mrs. B began dating a man with whom, a year after graduation, she established a marriage and a sex life she described as "pretty good" initially, but that soon came to feel routine, boring, and empty to her, as increasingly did her work life. Contraception had been abandoned for some time and Mrs. B became pregnant. Her marital sex life never seemed to recover after the birth of her son. For several years she lost her libido, and by the time her son was off to nursery school and then kindergarten, Mrs. B was becoming increasingly anhedonic, at times suffering from a low-grade depression. When Mrs. B eventually spoke of this to her family doctor, he prescribed an antidepressant and for a time this had seemed to help.

When, to her surprise, she found herself beginning to experience sexually arousing phantasies about women and attempting to use these phantasies to promote arousal in intercourse with her husband, she decided to enter therapy. Just prior to beginning her analytic psychotherapy, she had begun exploring chat groups of women with "bisexual" interests. Despite efforts to put this activity on hold, as advised by her analyst in order to get into the therapeutic process and exploration, she continued and, before long, had connected online to one particular woman. They soon graduated to email and then to the telephone and finally agreed to meet for coffee, and thus began Mrs. B's first extramarital affair.

She went off antidepressants, and her depression and anhedonia were, of course, a thing of the past, until this affair was broken off by her friend because she wanted more than Mrs. B was prepared to give her. Despite having loving as well as sexual feelings for her lover, and despite her unhappiness in her marriage, she loved both her son and her husband (albeit in a non-erotic sense) and was very attached to her home and her circle of friends, and couldn't contemplate the shame, disruption, and pain she anticipated bringing upon her immediate family and her very conventional parents if she were to "come out."

So she attempted to repress her homosexual interests and to throw herself back into her marriage, but it didn't work; her depression returned, at times making it difficult for her to function very well at all. Once again she began to feel better when she started flirting with and then secretly "date" other women, but this time these affairs seemed more superficial, more emotionally restricted, as Mrs. B appeared to have decided to remain in her marriage but from time to time to indulge in these limited homosexual connections.

It now became clear to Mrs. B that her "depression" was not neurochemically caused, as she had wanted to believe, but rather grounded in both sexual repression and in guilt about cheating on her husband, depriving him of a normal sex life, and living a lie. She not only had to hide all evidence of her extramarital activities but had to control her gaze and her interest in women when in the presence of her husband, family, and friends

Despite several years of analytic work on Mrs. B's internalized homophobia, her heterosexist superego, she finally decided she was not prepared to renovate her life. As she moved to termination, she expressed gratitude to the analyst for helping her achieve self-understanding: that her unhappiness was not the result of a bio-logically based depression, nor due exclusively to her heterosexist superego and internalized homophobia, but was also the price she was paying for choosing to continue to live a life of deceit and the guilt resulting from this choice.

I think in many analyses there comes an existential turning-point at which some patients find themselves equipped to begin to actualize the true self (Winnicott, 1965a), at whatever painful cost to themselves and others, while others are unable to do so, feeling forced to settle for less and, as a result, opting for lives of "quiet desperation." Often we can only speculate about the childhood conditions and possible constitutional strengths and weaknesses that enable some to refind, resurrect, and strengthen themselves – not least by reconciling with conscience – while others find them-selves unwilling or unable to do so.

Chapter 6

Recent contributions to the theory of the superego, guilt, and conscience

In his neglected classic, *Freud, Women and Morality: The Psychology of Good and Evil* (1988), the psychoanalytic sociologist Eli Sagan elaborated a theory of conscience and superego as distinct psychic functions developing in different ways and at different times. Whereas Freud viewed conscience as one of the three functions of the superego (the others being self-observation and maintenance of the ego-ideal) and saw it as arising at around five years of age with the shattering of the Oedipus complex due to fear of castration by the rival, Sagan posited a pre-Oedipal origin of conscience grounded in the infant's love for, and identification with, the primary nurturer.

Although Klein is not central to Sagan's theorizing, her work supports his general argument. Kleinians have long distinguished persecutory guilt, which amounts to self-torment, from depressive guilt, which, instead of being all about the self (as in shame and self-persecution), is about caring for and making reparation to the other. The dating of the move from the paranoid-schizoid and narcissistic position into the depressive position and the capacity for concern is controversial, but there is no doubt that conscience, as depressive position concern for the other, arises far earlier than the Freudian superego. The Kleinian view, like Sagan's, is now supported by empirical infant research on "the moral life of babies" (Bloom, 2010) that clearly indicates the pre-Oedipal roots of moral functioning.

As Sagan pointed out, it has long been difficult to comprehend how a mental function (the superego) formed from aggression

DOI: 10.4324/9781003347514-6

turned back against the self under the threat of castration, and operating, in Freud's (1930) words, "like a garrison in a conquered city" (p. 123), could be the seat of conscientious concern for others. For Sagan, where the superego is fuelled by hate, the conscience is grounded in attachment and love.

Sagan illustrates the distinction between conscience and superego by citing Mark Twain's depiction of "Huck's dilemma": his superego demands that he turn in his runaway slave companion Jim to the authorities, while his conscience requires him to protect his friend. While Freud understood that in addition to comprising aggression against the self, the superego is formed through internalization of the culture, he failed to fully appreciate the fact that the culture it internalized has generally been racist, sexist, heterosexist, etc.

Drawing on Lifton's (1986) work on the Nazi doctors, Sagan points out that they were, for the most part, not psychopaths but severely misguided idealists: they did their work, as Sagan would say, "under the banner of the superego," as did those who laboured in "the killing fields" of Cambodia under the Khmer Rouge, or dropped atom bombs on civilian populations. As I have argued elsewhere (Carveth, 2010), psychoanalysts have been so inclined to find the roots of human destructiveness in the id, the alleged "beast" in us, that we have grossly failed to recognize its roots in the uniquely human superego. A rebel cries, "Is this humanity? The oppressors are like animals!" To which I reply, "Is this animality? The oppressors are like humans!"

Against the immoral moralism of the superego, Alexander (1925) and Ferenczi, (1927/1928), like Bion (1962) more recently, grounded true morality in *thinking*. They viewed conscience as a rational ego function in which one thinks through the consequences of one's actions for oneself and others. In contrast to such rationalism, Sagan recognized that conscience arises not from *reason* but from *feeling*, from what Jean-Jacques Rousseau called "pity" – sympathy or fellow-feeling – "an innate abhorrence to see beings suffer that resemble him" (Rousseau, 1754, ch. 2).

For Sagan, whereas the superego arises through *identification with the aggressor* and operates essentially in accordance with the talion law of revenge ("an eye for an eye"), conscience arises through *identification with the nurturer* and operates through an analogous reciprocity, only one in which one feels called upon to return love for love received.

Herman Westerink's (2013) *A Dark Trace: Sigmund Freud on the Sense of Guilt* seeks to offer an account of Freud's evolving conceptualization of the sense of guilt. Although it does not claim to do more than describe "a dark trace" in Freud's work, it seems odd to read a contemporary publication that might well have been written in the 1940s. The book manages to go slightly beyond Freud's own work on the sense of guilt, briefly addressing in the penultimate chapter the controversies stimulated by Melanie Klein, Karen Horney, and others surrounding the pre-Oedipal phase, the role of the mother, and the psychology of women. But over five decades have passed since these controversies took place and many important contributions to this subject, such as Sagan's, are entirely neglected here.

Greater familiarity with the wider literature in the field might have spared the author some embarrassment. For example, ignoring the extensive critical literature pertaining to Freud's (1905) "Dora" case, Westerink describes it as "a vivid portrait of a complicated, passionate relationship in a decent, bourgeois environment," when "decent" is probably the last word one would use to describe Dora's family situation, in which her father attempts to bribe the husband of the woman with whom he is having an adulterous affair by offering him his daughter. Freud implicitly colludes with this attempted "swap," considering Dora's objections to the arrangement as symptoms of hysterical sexual inhibition.

In *You Ought To! A Psychoanalytic Study of the Superego and Conscience*, Bernard Barnett (2007) provides a good introductory overview of the contributions of not only Freud, but also Klein, Fairbairn, Winnicott, Bion, and many others in this area, and does so from the standpoint of one who has struggled clinically with the issues at hand. Barnett's discussion of guilt, superego, and conscience is enhanced by case illustrations from his own practice and by recurrent references to characters and themes drawn from George Eliot's classic novel, *Daniel Deronda*.

Although neglectful of the American literature, Barnett offers an even-handed survey, explanation, and illustration of central concepts in the field that will be useful for graduate students and beginning candidates in analytic training. But his book is in no way a critical, penetrating, or original study. In fact, the first note of criticism does not appear until some 40 pages into the text, at a point where it can hardly be avoided in favour of a simple exposition that Freud's infamous theory of the defective female superego is being reviewed.

Despite distinguishing conscience and superego in the subtitle of his book, in contrast to Freud treating them as largely synonymous, Barnett fails to face, think through, and elaborate clearly upon the distinction. In places he seems to consider conscience as a conscious moral function in contrast to the superego as the unconscious conscience, but he does not clearly spell this out or adhere to it consistently. In my view, this is just as well since the voice of conscience, like that of the superego, may be repressed. Barnett makes no reference to Sagan's distinction between the superego and the conscience, in which the superego is grounded in identification with the aggressor and fuelled by aggression, while the conscience is grounded in identification with the early nurturer and motivated by attachment and love.

It can only be the socially uncritical, bourgeois attitudes of mainstream psychoanalysis that account for the fact that, in the course of discussing the role of internalization in superego formation, Barnett, like most psychoanalysts, is largely blind to what should be obvious: the superego will inevitably function as the agent of cultural ideology – of racism, sexism, classism, heterosexism, and all the other forms of domination and immorality pervading the culture – at least to the extent that it is not opposed by a conscience having some degree of autonomy from the culture.

In the course of discussing the superego as a mischief-maker – the role of the severe superego in psychopathology – Barnett mentions identification with the punitive superego rationalizing aggression toward the other, the scapegoat, onto whom the subject's guilt has been projected. But he tends to see the severe or sadistic superego as entailing the "corruption of the superego systems . . . (i.e., a reversal of normal civilized values)" (p. 116), whereas history provides plenty of evidence that the socially normal superego is itself both corrupt (i.e., sexist, classist, etc.) and tyrannical, and that a humane and loving conscience is the exception rather than the rule. Freud himself, as we know, thought much of what appears as "moral" behaviour is pseudo-moral, grounded in social anxiety rather than genuinely felt values (Freud, 1933, p. 60):

> The stars are indeed magnificent, but as regards conscience God has done an uneven and careless piece of work, for a large majority of men have brought along with them only a modest amount of it or scarcely enough to be worth mentioning.

Barnett, like most analysts, views the developmental transformation of the primitive, harsh superego into a more humane and reasonable conscience as a process of superego modification analogous to the sort of piecemeal social reform preferred by liberals. In contrast, Freud himself, together with Franz Alexander and Sándor Ferenczi, took a revolutionary view in which it was not a matter of modification but rather of the "demolition" (Freud) or "elimination" (Ferenczi) of the superego altogether.

Whereas Freud, Alexander, and Ferenczi sought to replace the superego with the rational ego, viewing *thinking* as the foundation of moral function, Eli Sagan, like Pascal and Rousseau, rejects such rationalism, understanding that reason cannot specify value judgment. They recognize the foundation of conscience in feelings of empathic and sympathetic identification with the other, grounded in early identification with the nurturer. When the superego (identification with the aggressor) is deconstructed or relatively disempowered it can no longer drown out the voice of conscience (identification with the nurturer).

For Sagan, Freud's deficient understanding of the roots of conscience arises from his deficient psychology of women; more specifically, his almost phobic theoretical flight forward to the Oedipal and away from the overwhelming (divine and demonic) pre-Oedipal maternal imago.

Oddly, in the course of his discussion of "blind obedience" among the Nazis, Barnett makes no reference to the classic studies on obedience by Milgram (1963) that experimentally validate Freud's (1921) concept of the usurpation of individual conscience by an authoritative leader. Barnett's easy use of terms such as *normal* and *healthy* to describe the type of superego he values, and *criminal* for the type he devalues, reflects little more than uncritical bourgeois ideology.

Despite his useful discussion of the SS, Lifton's (1986) work on the Nazi doctors and the mechanisms of "psychic numbing" and "doubling" that enabled them to split off an "Auschwitz self" from the self they resumed at home, Barnett does not fully grasp the fact that their abominable work was enabled and driven by the superego. The tendency to find the roots of evil in the id, rather than the superego, is deeply ingrained in psychoanalytic thought. But as a survivor friend of Lifton's (1986, p. 5) remarked, "It is demonic that they were not demonic!" That is, it is horrifying that they were, for the most part, not id-driven psychopaths but superego-driven ideologues.

It is not as if Barnett is oblivious to the role of the superego in such behaviour: he views it as a "criminal" or "pathological" superego, and this allows him to continue to think that "in health" the "normal" superego is humane. Thus, he dodges the uncomfortable truth that *normally* the superego is not humane, which is why it comes into conflict with the conscience, provided the conscience can make itself heard over the ideological clamour of the superego.

Barnett offers a useful discussion of the superego dynamics of Holocaust survivors and the transmission of their pathologies to the next generation. To his credit, in the final chapter he discusses a range of post-Freudian approaches, reviewing the work of Klein, Winnicott, Fairbairn (on the "moral defence"), and Bion, as well as such thinkers as Foucault, Kristeva, Zygmunt Bauman, and Slavoj Žižek. As one who clearly grasps the pathology of the normal superego, Žižek sees advanced consumer capitalism as fuelling our narcissism and undermining our freedom, not by commanding us to work, but rather by insisting that we "enjoy!"

Like Barnett, Annie Reiner (2009) is a practising psychoanalyst, a former student of Bion's. James Grotstein writes a useful foreword to her book in which he praises what he sees as the originality of her distinction between the superego and the conscience and her view of their separate lines of development. There is no recognition by either Grotstein or Reiner of Eli Sagan's development of this very distinction some two decades earlier, or of the contributions of Fromm (1947, 1950), Jung (1958), or Symington (1994) in this area.

Unlike Sagan who, like Klein and Winnicott, grounds conscience (as distinct from the critical superego) in early feelings of love and concern rather than in reason, Reiner follows Bion in finding the basis for conscientious development beyond the rigid, pseudo-moral superego in *thinking*. For such thinking to occur it is necessary, she believes, for the subject to experience a "psychological birth" beyond the merely physical one, a "resurrection" of the true self that has early on been split off in favour of false self-development due to virtually universal deficiencies of containment by the early nurturers.

Such metaphors of "second birth" and "resurrection" suggest the author's embrace of a type of "spirituality" that she, like Symington (1994) and others, distinguishes from conventional forms of religiosity. In her view there is false, literalistic religion and there is true, sophisticated spirituality. Reiner goes so far as to affirm Nietzsche's notion of the "Superman" – Grotstein prefers "Overman" and "Higher Man" (not "Higher Woman"?). She calls us to advance "beyond good and evil," as conventionally defined (the superego's pseudo-morality), toward the more highly evolved, "authentic" spirituality of those special people (Mystics, Messiahs, etc.) who have managed to cast off their false selves and experience a "transformation in O" – O being defined as "ultimate reality, absolute truth, the godhead, the infinite, the thing-in-itself" (Bion, 1970, p. 25).

It is easy enough to engage in this not-so-subtly self-congratulatory sort of talk in which the "inner truth" of religion, demythologized and interpreted in existential and psychoanalytic terms, is distinguished from its "falsely reified and concretized forms" – that is, from the "common man's" magical and literal faith. But such "spiritual" interpretations of religion as metaphor referring to "the absolute" or "the godhead" or "O" – of "Higher Men," "Mystics," and "Messiahs" – smacks, frankly, of the kind of grandiosity that bedevils spiritual traditions and that leads some to speak of "the stink of enlightenment."

Regrettably, in addition to following Bion in his mysticism, Reiner is uncritical of his peculiar type of Neoplatonic rationalism that posits "the thought without a thinker" (Reiner, p. 8). Is "the proto-mental realm" the place where unthought thoughts patiently await the arrival of a thinker to think them? Is this to all intents and purposes "the mind of God"?

Reiner posits that it is through a process of spiritual development that the false self is overcome and the true self is resurrected, that the subject may acquire the capacity to think and to encounter and bear truth, and so develop a maturing conscience. In this view, authentic conscience (as distinct from superego) is a spiritual attainment of one who evolves "beyond good and evil." While Eli Sagan also sees the necessity to distinguish conscience from superego, his view of the matter, like Melanie Klein's, is developed entirely in secular humanist and psychological terms. Following both Klein and Sagan, we can say that while conscience does develop into more complex and sophisticated forms as maturation occurs, it is there virtually from the beginning in the infant's simple preference for pleasure (good) over pain (bad) and in its love for the nurturing good part-object breast and, later, good whole-object mother.

Harold Searles (1975) pointed out that infants will put their own needs and development on the back burner and devote themselves to attempting to cure their depressed or anxious mothers – not merely out of a need to get her to straighten up and fly right so as to provide the mothering they need or a need to make reparation to her for aggressive feelings and phantasies, but also out of sheer dumb love and the simple desire to make her happy. Reiner follows Bion in his rationalistic valourization of thinking over loving.

For Sagan, conscience is grounded in the infant's love for the mother who has loved and nurtured it and in its wish to love her back. We can expect to find the mature operation of such conscience not only in the conceits of "spirituality" but also in moral and political concern and commitment to oppose and remedy the evils and injustices of the world. Despite the Enlightenment atheism Sagan shares with Freud, his perspective is congruent with that element of the Christian outlook that locates goodness in a peasant babe in a manger before whom sophisticated philosopher-kings ("Higher Men") fall on their knees. Christianity was seldom surprised to find the demonic among sophisticated "thinkers" or simple goodness in the "Holy Fool."

While Reiner fails to acknowledge Sagan's priority, she implicitly validates his distinction between superego and conscience. In addition, she advances our understanding by insightfully applying Winnicott's (1960) true self/false self theory, correctly associating conscience with development of the true self and recognizing, with Fairbairn (1952), how this is almost universally derailed for, as Reiner puts it, "that which we generally consider to be a 'good-enough mother' may not be good enough" (p. 125).

Through the process Fairbairn called "the moral defence," the inadequately contained and nurtured child blames itself for the parental failures, since "it is better to be a sinner in a world ruled by God than to live in a world ruled by the Devil" (Fairbairn, 1952, p. 66; quoted by Reiner, 2009, p. 69). This defence lays the basis for major moral confusion: what is bad is good and what is good is bad; what is true is false and what is false is true. One has now lost one's existential compass.

Feelings arising from the true self, especially aggression in reaction to parental failure, are split off; the unconscious aggression fuels the hostile superego. But whereas Reiner thinks that in these circumstances conscience, like the true self, fails to develop, I think it is repressed but still in existence and that it generates an existentially valid sense of guilt distinct from that generated by the superego: an existential guilt, if you will, a guilt for failing to be one's self, for failing to *be*, and for being false.

One of the great strengths of Reiner's book is the extensive, detailed, and convincing case material she provides, which, since she is a talented and lucid writer, wonderfully demonstrates both her clinical acumen and the validity of a good deal of her thinking. This is an important book; it contains some false notes but also a great deal of truth.

However much our thinking may correspond with inner and outer reality, it is profoundly shaped by the socio-economic substructure. This is as true of psychoanalytic thought as of any other. While "the culture of narcissism" (Lasch, 1979) created by consumer capitalism put the study of narcissistic pathology on our agenda, it simultaneously infected us with it, giving rise to our five-decade-long "forgetting" of the superego and of what, with Sagan (1988), I distinguish as the conscience (Carveth, 2013).

In *Reshaping the Psychoanalytic Domain: The Work of Melanie Klein, W. R. D. Fairbairn, and D. W. Winnicott*, Judith Hughes (1989) surveyed the emergence of psychoanalytic object-relations theory. In *Guilt and Its Vicissitudes* (Hughes, 2008) she focuses in depth upon the evolving understanding of morality in the work of Freud himself and that of Melanie Klein and her various followers who further developed it (Hanna Segal, Joan Riviere, Wilfred Bion, Betty Joseph, John Steiner, Ronald Britton, and others). A historian by training, Hughes writes about psychoanalytic ideas not only with scholarly depth and sophistication but also with a clinician's understanding of the issues.

Having carefully reviewed the development of Freud's thinking in this area, Hughes then traces the development of Klein's important contributions and those of her collaborators (Riviere, Segal) who, despite their innovations, remain close to her own understanding, and then the more recent work of contemporary Kleinians influenced by Bion (Joseph, Steiner, and Britton), who shift significantly in their thinking about morality, stressing less the role of love in the ambivalence of the depressive position in generating concern and reparative guilt and more the role in moral functioning of cognitive development and the capacity to think. Thus, in the course of her survey, Hughes manages to highlight important theoretical tensions that remain controversial today. As someone who has recently come down on the Kleinian rather than the Bionian side in this debate (Carveth, 2013), my only regret is that Hughes ultimately roots for the wrong team – the thinkers rather than the lovers.

According to Freud (1933), "Our best hope for the future is that intellect – the scientific spirit, reason – may in process of time establish a dictatorship in the mental life of man" (p. 170). Given such rationalism (Freud's wish to establish a dictatorship of the ego over the id and superego, as if an ego-dominated person could be anything more than a pathological narcissist or a psychopath), the neo-Kleinian shift from an emphasis upon loving concern for the other to a stress upon thinking and reality-testing (as if that could ever tell us right from wrong) represents a regression from Klein's hard-won advance beyond both the father in and the father of psychoanalysis.

Although Hughes comments upon the essentially sociological nature of Freud's understanding of the superego as grounded in fear of rejection and consequent introjection of and identification with social authority via the parents' superegos, she does not elaborate upon the problems of moral relativism this generates. Although he advanced a view of morality mostly as socially constructed, in "Totem and Taboo" Freud, (1912–1913) described the remorse stemming from the killing of the ambivalently loved primal father that led to the establishment of the moral law in the first place. In Freud's historical myth (and implied in his account of the Oedipal development of the individual), guilt, instead of resulting from the superego, precedes and motivates its formation.

Hughes does not really address the contradiction in Freud's thought between views of guilt as a cause and as a result of superego development. However, she correctly notes that Klein's thinking about moral development builds upon the primordial ambivalence that leads to guilt for hating an object that is also loved and, hence, to reparative wishes. In other words, guilt has its deepest roots in a love/hate conflict intrinsic to human nature, whatever additional guilt we derive from socialization into particular cultures.

Hughes is to be congratulated for calling attention to important aspects of Melanie Klein's thinking – such as her insistence upon the role of guilt due to ambivalence even in psychotic conditions wherein it may be so deeply buried or split off as to be virtually invisible (Hughes, 2008, p. 64). Certainly, analysts schooled in relational, self, and intersubjective approaches focused upon attuning empathically to conscious and preconscious experience will remain oblivious to its presence in psychosis and also in psychopathy and other narcissistic states in which depressive, as distinct from persecutory, anxiety is warded off by a range of essentially manic defences, as Joan Riviere so well understood, as Hughes points out.

In relation to the cognitive turn in post-Kleinian thought, Hughes quotes (p. 82) from a note by Klein to Susan Isaacs in which she indicates what she feels is the latter's overemphasis upon unconscious phantasy, to the relative neglect of the primitive ego's interest in and influence by reality. Hanna Segal responded to this concern, evolving a more balanced perspective that does greater justice to ego development and to what Freudians call primary and secondary process thinking, which Segal associates with symbolic equation and symbolic representation, respectively. In so attending to the development and pathology of the ego and its capacity to think and test reality, Segal in no way departs from the classical Kleinian stress on the role of object love in the ambivalence that generates concern and reparation and that motivates symbolism and sublimation.

By way of contrast to this classical Kleinian stress upon the growth-promoting role of the *subject's* love, Bion's emphasis upon the role of the containing *object* in enabling thinking and learning from experience seems to have contributed to an unfortunate post-Kleinian preoccupation with the role of *thinking* in moral development – unfortunate because as both Jean-Jacques Rousseau (1754) and Melanie Klein understood, morality is grounded not in thinking but in *feeling*. For Rousseau this was fellow-feeling or *pity;* for Klein it was feelings of love and gratitude toward the good object.

As Hughes herself recognizes, this post-Kleinian emphasis upon the role of thinking in morality runs into difficulty in view of the fact/value disjunction: one cannot deduce an "ought" from an "is"; science is *descriptive* not *prescriptive*; we can reason from value premises, but reason is incapable of authorizing or validating such premises. Hughes seeks to offset her well-justified anxiety in this respect by referencing in a footnote (p. 120) a recent philosophical study claiming to have undermined the fact/value disjunction but that, in my judgment, merely complicates it to some degree. A good deal of modern philosophy seeks to complicate established axioms, sometimes giving the impression they have been overcome when, in reality, they have merely been complicated. In light of such complication, the axiom may now seem unsophisticated. But sophistry has always sought through complication to baffle reason. It is true that clear thinking about facts is *relevant* to moral functioning: the fact that smoking causes cancer is relevant to my decision whether or not to smoke. But the fact that smoking may impair my health and shorten my life in no way proves that it is better to be healthy than ill, nor that life is worth living. Those are judgments beyond reason; they are grounded not in the subject's thinking but in *Eros* – in the subject's love or lack thereof.

In *The Anatomy of Regret: From Death Instinct to Reparation and Symbolization through Vivid Case Studies*, Susan Kavaler-Adler (2013) presents the revised version of Kleinian theory, integrated with concepts of Fairbairn, Winnicott, and Mahler, that informs her view of the therapeutic process as one of "developmental mourning." It is through facing up to and mourning one's destructiveness (arising in Kavaler-Adler's view not from innate aggression but from trauma broadly defined) and one's consequent regrets, all in the context of a therapeutic holding environment, that one is able to liberate oneself from one's defensive and maladaptive "false self" (Winnicott), one's "antilibidinal ego" or "internal saboteur" (Fairbairn), and from Freud's and Klein's sadistic superego. Having clearly outlined her theoretical framework, the author illustrates it through a series of richly described case studies which, to my mind, succeed in demonstrating in clinical detail her theory in practice and its therapeutic power in work with patients suffering from diverse levels and types of psychopathology.

Kavaler-Adler's perspective is very similar to my own, as outlined in *The Still Small Voice: Psychoanalytic Reflections on Guilt and Conscience* (Carveth, 2013). Whereas I speak more about guilt than regret, the two are really inseparable as one cannot genuinely face and learn how to bear one's guilt without at the same time experiencing regret about the damage one has done to others and to oneself. Kavaler-Adler and I agree with Melanie

Klein that consciously integrating one's guilt and regret, working through the depressive position and moving toward reparation is the path toward recovery. But because I have a narrower concept of mourning than Kavaler-Adler's, restricting it to working through losses, including those resulting from our destructiveness, I do not conceptualize genuinely facing guilt and regret as mourning *per se*. Though certainly sobering and humbling, moving into and working through the depressive position relieves one from painful alienation, shame, and superego torment and promotes reconciliation with conscience. I suspect some patients on the verge of the depressive position who intensely and extensively experience mournfulness and what Kavaler-Adler calls "the grief of regret" may be using these persecutory states as a delaying tactic, a defence against genuine progress through getting on with the work of repentance and reparation.

While many deplore the fragmented state of contemporary psychoanalysis, I see the fragments as pieces of a wonderfully complex puzzle that we are gradually beginning to be able to piece together and which will constitute the higher dialectical synthesis of the existing partial perspectives. In this connection it is relevant to note Kavaler-Adler's (2014) latest title, *The Klein-Winnicott Dialectic: Transformative New Metapsychology and Interactive Clinical Theory*. Analysts who have immersed themselves in Freud, Klein, Fairbairn, Winnicott, Mahler, Kohut, and others appear to be breaking out of their theoretical tunnels, overcoming tunnel-vision, and glimpsing and beginning to delineate an overarching framework for psychoanalysis. In this connection, a recent posting by Arnold Richards (2014) to the *Clio's Psyche* psychohistory listserv is of interest: "A worldwide conceptual survey by the IPA shows that the number one and number two concepts were transference/countertransference and projective identification," a finding he feels "supports the view that there is a new conceptual consensus with a Kleinian take." Kavaler-Adler is an important contributor to this emerging synthesis.

In working out her object relational synthesis, Kavaler-Adler felt it necessary to offer a critique of Klein's acceptance of Freud's concept of the death drive because, without denying the potential role of innate temperamental differences and mismatches between infants and their carers, she views significant psychopathology as arising not from universal biological forces but from traumatic deprivation, frustration, impingement, and abuse. While I share her rejection of the concept of a literal death instinct (though this term is employed in such radically different ways by different authors that it is only in specific contexts that one can hope to know what they might mean by it), Kavaler-Adler fails to draw attention to the fact that on almost every page where Klein mentions projection of the death instinct to account for the inevitable persecutory anxiety of even the most sensitively cared-for infant, she at the same time offers an alternate, and to me, far more acceptable explanation: namely, that given its cognitive limitations the infant is bound to misinterpret every frustration as an attack and, hence, that the absent good breast is felt as a present bad attacking breast. In "The Origins of Transference," Klein (1952, p. 433) writes:

These persecutory feelings from inner sources are intensified by painful external experiences, for, from the earliest days onwards, frustration and discomfort arouse in the infant the feeling that he is being attacked by hostile forces. Therefore the sensations experienced by the infant at birth and the difficulties of adapting himself to entirely new conditions give rise to persecutory anxiety. The comfort and care given after birth, particularly the first feeding experiences, are felt to come from good forces.

Like many North American analysts, Kavaler-Adler appears to have bought into the idea that Klein ignored or minimized the role of the real parenting in health and pathology, perhaps influenced, as so many have been, by John Bowlby's slanderous claims in this regard (see references and discussion in Carveth, 2013, ch. 9). In actuality, Klein constantly stressed the crucial importance of good, loving care-taking, for only this can hope to offset the inevitable rage and paranoia resulting from frustration, both that which is basic and unavoidable and the surplus frustration arising from parental failure in varying degrees. In "Mourning and its Relation to Manic-Depressive States," Klein (1940, p. 128) writes:

> All the enjoyments which the baby lives through in relation to his mother are so many proofs to him that the loved object inside as well as outside is not injured, is not turned into a vengeful person. The increase of love and trust, and the diminishing of fears through happy experiences, help the baby step by step to overcome his depression and feeling of loss (mourning). They enable him to test his inner reality by means of outer reality. Through being loved and through the enjoyment and comfort he has in relation to people his confidence in his own as well as in other people's goodness becomes strengthened, his hope that his "good" objects and his own ego can be saved and preserved increases, at the same time as his ambivalence and acute fears of internal destruction diminish. Unpleasant experiences and the lack of enjoyable ones, in the young child, especially lack of happy and close contact with loved people, increase ambivalence, diminish trust and hope and confirm anxieties about inner annihilation and external persecution; moreover they slow down and perhaps permanently check the beneficial processes through which in the long run inner security is achieved.

For the reasons indicated, Klein's references to the concept of the death drive are redundant and can safely be ignored, since she always provided another far more acceptable explanation of the same set of facts. Since Klein considered the parents' provision of loving experiences as crucial for development, it cannot be said that she sought to get them off the hook, as it were, blaming pathology entirely on the child's drives and phantasies. Hence, there is no need for Kavaler-Adler's speculative psychoanalysis of Klein's alleged motives for doing so (such as needing to engage in a Fairbairnian "moral defence" of her mother by blaming herself and the drives and phantasies of children in general) for, in reality, she never denied the role of the real caretakers in development in the first place.

Despite some differences with Kavaler-Adler in the ways indicated above, I believe her work represents an important contribution to the integrative psychoanalytic theory that is beginning to emerge after decades of fragmentation of our field into an array of partial and non-interacting perspectives. One of her book's major strengths is its many detailed and extensive case studies that will prove invaluable to students and colleagues seeking a practical, clinically grounded understanding of her conceptual and clinical approach.

In Guilt: Origins, Manifestations, and Management

Salman Akhtar (2013) has, as editor, collected three papers delivered at the 43rd Annual Margaret S. Mahler Symposium on Child Development (Philadelphia, April 28, 2012), together with three response papers, an introductory overview, and a concluding commentary. Of the spate of books that have emerged recently representing the return of the topic of guilt from repression for over four decades in psychoanalysis, this is by far the best from a clinical, as well as a theoretical, point of view. The papers by William Singletary, Desy Safán-Gerard, and Stanley Coen, together with Elio Frattaroli's discussion of Coen and elaboration of his own important ideas regarding the absence of morality in psychoanalytic theory and practice, are each in their own way gems of clinical and theoretical psychoanalytic insight.

In his introductory overview, Akhtar addresses a range of important conceptual issues, seeking to clarify distinctions between guilt, shame, regret, and remorse. He helpfully outlines the different varieties of guilt (annihilation, epistemic, Oedipal, separation, induced, deposited, survivor's) and varying consequences of guilt, both pathological (its projection, externalization, and libidinization) and healthy (seeking forgiveness and making reparation). In many areas of psychoanalytic theory, confusion arises from the fact that key concepts and terms are understood in very different ways. While many will agree that "shame is developmentally earlier than guilt" (p. 3), not all will agree that guilt "in its true meaning only evolves after the post-oedipal consolidation of the superego" (p. 3). For Melanie Klein (1948), persecutory guilt is normally supplemented by depressive anxiety or reparative guilt on entry into the depressive position, long before the consolidation of the Freudian superego at five or six years of age. Akhtar acknowledges that Klein uses the terms *guilt* and *remorse* interchangeably. For this reason, few Kleinians would agree that "guilt is about breaking rules and remorse about hurting others" (p. 4), holding instead that remorse is a type of depressive (as distinct from persecutory) guilt and that one might well experience remorse and regret over breaking rules and so injuring the moral community espousing them. While Akhtar's overview reflects a more Freudian orientation, several other contributors to this volume parallel the Kleinian view in differentiating between "good" (reparative) and "bad" (persecutory) guilt. Akhtar offers a helpful discussion of the technical handling of guilt as it emerges during clinical sessions.

William Singletary's "Pinocchio's Journey to a Good Heart: Guilt, Reparation, and Transformation" (2013) views Carlo Collodi's (1883) story as an allegory of the process of emancipation from serious psychopathology and offers a moving account of the 16-year treatment of a boy originally diagnosed with Asperger's whose development clearly illustrates this process. Like the figures in the lower rungs of Dante's *Inferno* who are frozen in ice and unable to move, at the beginning Pinocchio is a notably motherless, hostile, self-centred, and callous spirit imprisoned in a block of wood. He is indifferent to and unappreciative of his loving father and rejects good and helpful figures like the Cricket (the "still small voice of conscience") and the positively guiding Blue Fairy, seduced instead by delinquent figures into a magical and omnipotent world of self-indulgence. In the face of his father's illness and suffering, Pinocchio gradually changes direction, working to heal his father and in the process developing a "good heart" and finally becoming, as his father had wished, "a real boy." Singletary distinguishes the "good conscience" that promotes love and responsibility from the "bad conscience" (i.e., hostile and corrupt superego) that both seduces and punishes.

Singletary points out that when the normal developmental process of giving and receiving love is seriously derailed, love becomes threatening and defences are set up against it. "A five-year-old boy impulsively jumped from the top stair in my toy closet. I caught him, preventing his injury, and his response was to spit in my face!" (p. 18). When, after a wonderful time with his mother, the patient immediately kicked her, Singletary said to him, "I think that whenever you're mean to people, it's because you're feeling more loving and caring toward them" (p. 17). He sees "interpretation of hatred as a reaction to feeling more love rather than as a justified reaction to hurt" (p. 18) as central to transforming hate back into love and thus promoting "good guilt" and the drive toward reparation. This understanding of hostility, omnipotence, and withdrawal as defences against the threat constituted by love and need is crucial in work not only with children on the autism spectrum but with all those who resort to narcissistic defences against the dangers constituted by object love: need, dependency, rejection, and loss. Significantly, in this connection Singletary describes another patient's "descent into Asperger's" (p. 23), viewing this condition as constructed as a defence against psychic pain.

In "Bearable and Unbearable Guilt: A Kleinian Perspective," Desy Safán-Gerard offers a remarkably open, detailed, and illuminating account of four back-to-back sessions with a narcissistic, guilt-evading man. Correctly understanding her work to be not that of liberating the patient from an unreasonably harsh superego but rather as helping him to begin to be able to bear the justified guilt arising from his destructiveness, her initial attempts to interpret his defences against guilt succeed only in involving her in a sado-masochistic transference and counter-transference. The patient then uses what appears to him to be (and, in all honesty, is) the analyst's scolding to expiate rather than learn how to bear his guilt, just as he does through a range of self-defeating behaviours. In other words, his evasion of justified guilt only strengthens his sadistic superego, which, with the analyst's assistance through her scolding interpretations, he projects onto her as a now-external persecutor. But the ongoing self-monitoring of this experienced analyst begins to alert her to what is going on. She begins to recognize her guilt for the scolding interpretations and how she has been punishing herself by allowing the patient to accrue a debt. In light of this growing understanding, by the third session she is remembering that the patient's guilt is a measure of his love for his objects, and she begins to shift her technique away from interpreting defences against guilt toward drawing attention to the love underlying the guilt. She begins to convey empathic understanding of the intense pain with which the patient is threatened if he acknowledges his callous behaviour toward his loved objects. Safán-Gerard is to be complimented for her courage in providing us with a remarkably honest account of the counter-transference, enactments, and errors that she came to recognize and correct.

Just as Singletary's patient spits in his face after he saves him from injury and another boy kicks his mother after a particularly lovely day with her, so Safán-Gerard's patient wonders "why he should go after another woman *precisely* after having made love to Alma" (p. 53). She writes, "The awareness of such love makes the patient acutely aware of his or her separateness and infantile dependence on the object that he or she is manically trying to deny" (p. 44). By the fourth session, after his analyst has made great strides in overcoming her counter-transference and re-establishing empathic contact with her patient's pain, her patient remarks, "I can't believe I *did* that!" and ends the session saying, "This is very sad . . . this is very painful." Safán-Gerard offers us very important advice on work with narcissistic patients: the analyst needs "to bring the patient's attention to that moment in the session where guilt was experienced, acknowledging how painful it must be to recognize neglect or damage toward loved ones or toward the self" (p. 56). "Mobilizing the love might have prevented a sado-masochistic enactment in the transference" (p. 57). In Kleinian fashion, Safán-Gerard points out that this patient's difficulty in moving fully into a depressive position concern for his objects is due to "his unconscious envy and jealousy which makes him want to spoil and devalue them" (p. 57). I would like to suggest that whatever primary basis they may or may not have, such envy and jealousy are, in my experience, at least inflamed, if not caused, by the perception that the good objects are *unwilling to share*, that they are withholding their goodness, or that they are simply in one way or another absent or "dead." Interpreting this as the basis of destructive envy is another way to be experienced by the patient as empathic rather than judgmental.

In "Guilt in the Therapist and Its Impact upon Treatment," Stanley Coen (2013) encourages colleagues both to scan themselves and to identify with analysts in trouble. Instead of dissociating ourselves from such colleagues, insisting that, unlike them, we are well enough analyzed and trained to avoid such problems, he suggests we should face the more threatening task of focusing on our own needs, vulnerabilities, and temptations that might lead us astray. In his view, "Some degree of anxiety and mistrust of ourselves seems essential for protecting the analytic situation" (p. 74). He wonders if it might be significant that when he presented "The Wish to Regress in Patient and Analyst," a discussant who insisted he had never had such temptations subsequently got into ethical trouble. For Coen, we need, as much as possible, to allow ourselves to be conscious of our unacceptable impulses and desires, while at the same time be able to contain and not be overwhelmed and drawn into acting on them. The optimal superego stance for the analyst at work involves scanning his needs, wishes, and temptations from the standpoint of an overseeing, guiding, criticizing, restraining, praising, and loving superego.

What Coen fails to mention is that this superego bears little resemblance to the superego Freud gave us, driven by castration fear and operating "like a garrison in a conquered city" (Freud, 1930, p. 123), but rather to the revisionist "loving and beloved" superego offered by Roy Schafer (1960) which, as I indicated earlier, is in my view not the superego at all. The "tolerant, loving attitude toward the analyst's affective experience" (p. 70) to which Coen refers is characteristic not of the superego but of what, following Sagan, I call the conscience (Carveth, 2013, 2015, 2016), a structure that, along with the ego-ideal, Freud (1923) merged with the superego, but that I argue is separate from and capable of conflicting with it. The kind of scanning or self-monitoring Coen recommends is a function not primarily of the superego but of the ego-ideal and the conscience – the latter requiring a "good heart," something that, unlike far too many psychoanalysts, Stanley Coen clearly possesses and uses to good effect.

In "Reflections on the Absence of Morality in Psychoanalytic Theory and Practice," Elio Frattaroli (2013) writes that Coen's method of listening and scanning is "the heart and soul of psychoanalysis," for it "gives us entry into the sacred space where healing can occur" (p. 85). But, he points out, "Considering the disturbingly high-incidence of sexual boundary violations among psychoanalysts, it is apparent that too many of us . . . don't do the kind of . . . self-scanning that Stanley Coen recommends" (p. 88) – namely self-scanning that is "*guided by a deeply moral sensibility*" (p. 87; original emphasis). Frattaroli validates the kind of "honest and thorough self-analysis of disturbing counter-transference impulses" illustrated in Coen's report of his work with Mr. R and points out that the kind of deep connectedness this can facilitate between analyst and analysand, far from promoting boundary violations, "always entails increased compassion, never increased desire" (p. 90).

By "the sacred space where healing can occur," Frattaroli is referring to Winnicott's area of play, "the creative space in which the spontaneous True Self is born" (p. 90). "To hold this space as sacred is an act of love. To ignore or violate it is an act of tyranny." Like Singletary (2013), who distinguishes "bad" and "good" conscience, and Klein, who distinguishes persecutory from depressive or reparative guilt, Frattaroli points to two varieties of contrition, one "where guilt is primarily a fear of Hell" and another in which it is "primarily a feeling of remorse for hurting someone you love" (p. 91). Here he also refers to Martin Buber's distinction between neurotic and authentic guilt, the former based on a fear of punishment for violation of parental and socially constructed rules and the latter "based in the reality of doing something we know is truly immoral" (p. 91). Here he points to the difference between Coen's "superego" (what I call conscience) and Freud's (p. 95):

> An analyst motivated by Freud's kind of superego would restrain himself from violating sexual boundaries not out of empathy and respect for the patient, but out of fear of what might happen to him if he did what he wanted. He wouldn't have clear knowledge that it is always wrong to have sex with a patient. He would know only that it is forbidden. Unlike the moral compass of our True Self, the Freudian superego remains like a foreign body or external voice in our heads that becomes part of our Winnicottian False Self.

The absence in Freudian theory of the idea of a guiding moral compass has, for Frattaroli, dangerous consequences. "It is a disturbing fact that nowhere in his writings does Freud suggest that it is morally wrong or even psychologically unhealthy to selfishly use other people for one's own sexual gratification" (p. 98). Frattaroli here recounts the dismal story of Freud's (1905) morally obtuse and inexcusable treatment of Dora, a 14-year-old girl essentially pimped out by her father to the husband of the woman with whom he was having an affair, a girl Freud diagnosed as hysterical for her refusal to go along with the perverse arrangement. Frattaroli asks (p. 101):

> So if Freud never recognized the immorality of a parent sexually abusing his own child, if he failed to recognize the immorality of his own self-serving misuse of Dora – as is evident from his lack of guilt and shame in publishing the details of how he understood and treated her – how then can we expect psychoanalysts who have been trained in the Freudian tradition to recognize the immorality of more subtle misuses of our patients? . . . I doubt there is a single psychoanalytic institute that currently teaches the Dora case for what it really is: a cautionary model of what psychoanalysis *at its worst* can be.
>
> (Emphasis original)

Frattaroli points out that in contrast to what Buber (1923) called "I-it" relations in which one uses or imposes oneself on others, in "I-Thou" relations one helps another to unfold. Following Summers (2001), he writes (p. 93):

The models of therapeutic action currently accepted in different schools of psychoanalytic thought – interpretation and insight, internalization of the analyst's self-psychological functions, or the impact of the real relationship with a collaborative co-constructing analyst – all emphasize, in one way or another what the (active) analyst must do or provide for the (passive) patient, and all fail to appreciate that the healing process is internally generated by the patient . . . and his innate tendency toward self-unfolding and actualization.

If the latter idea sounds excessively romantic or mystical to the psychoanalytic ear, Frattaroli reminds us that for Melanie Klein "the depressive position unfolds naturally out of the paranoid-schizoid position" and therefore, human beings "have an innate direction not only of sexual but of moral development; a direction that includes the innate moral tendency to feel remorse (authentic guilt) for wanting to harm someone we love" (p. 106).

In locating the roots of conscience (as distinct from superego) in Klein's "depressive anxiety," Winnicott's "capacity for concern," and in early attachment and identifications with good objects, I depart somewhat from Frattaroli's identification of conscience with what he calls our "higher consciousness" composed of the capacity for self-observation or self-reflection (as in Coen's self-scanning). Although Frattaroli does not cite the work of George Herbert Mead (1937) or the symbolic interactionist social psychologists who followed him, this tradition in American pragmatic philosophy and sociology also focused upon what it saw as our uniquely human capacity to imaginatively take the role of the other and then look back at ourselves as objects from the perspective of the other, as the basis of moral order. The problem is that this is a capacity that saints share with psychopaths who have to be skilled in precise empathy to be able to know how best to deceive and manipulate others. Empathy is not sympathy. To know that another is in pain is not at all the same thing as caring and wishing to help. The latter comes from prosocial feelings and attachments that we share with other primate species. In this light, what we humans need is not more of the "higher" consciousness so often expressed in our uniquely human destructiveness, but more of the "lower" consciousness we see in animal altruism (De Waal, 2013). Coen's (2013) method of self-scanning can be used for good or for ill. It will be used constructively only when it is informed by what Pinocchio finally achieved: a "good heart."

Chapter 7

Why I write about guilt

Elsewhere (Carveth, 2018, ch. 8) I have traced what I call the melancholic existentialism of Ernest Becker (1973) and the related melancholic social theory of Peter Berger (1965) to the unresolved depression that prevented them from seeing the splitting and the one-sidedness entailed in their attitudes of despair and disgust. Becker and his followers in "terror-management theory" have the idea that death anxiety is our primordial fear, the Ur-anxiety motivating the denial of death through the quest for immortality and various forms of heroism, just as Berger thinks we construct society and religion as illusory defences against what he takes to be the reality of chaos and anomy.

For these thinkers, in seeking to analyze and resolve defences, psychoanalysts threaten to expose the unbearable reality against which we must defend ourselves. Society, religions, and heroic projects of various sorts function as "shields against terror" without which we must go mad. By "existentializing" rather than psychologizing anxiety in these ways, grounding it in allegedly universal yet unbearable truth, these thinkers avoid having to consider what alternative, personal rather than impersonal, grounds there might be for their persecutory anxiety and depression. By blaming these states on the human condition, the absurdity and meaninglessness of life, they avoid having to consider other possible causes: "No, no, it's not because I'm cheating on my wife or my taxes, or mean or neglectful of my kids, or a self-centred egotist, racist, sexist, heterosexist or classist . . . no, it's *la condition humaine*. I don't need analysis to get at the deeper reasons

DOI: 10.4324/9781003347514-7

for my malaise, I just need better denial of death, better terror management – or maybe Paxil."

Underlying the variegated forms of suffering patients present – the hysterical and psychosomatic symptoms, the anxiety and depression, the patterns of self-limitation and self-sabotage – lie the real or imagined moral failings, character flaws, petty envy, greed and meanness, the death wishes toward others, the *schadenfreude*, and the outright crimes and misdemeanours that, in an earlier age prior to our culture of narcissism, people took it as the goal of their lives to combat, to struggle, to transcend. Certainly the critical superego can greatly exaggerate our flaws, even accusing us of crimes of which we are mostly innocent. And certainly the burden of guilt we carry may be undeserved, sometimes induced in us through projection by others who scapegoat us. But although we should oppose excessive and unjustified self-reproach, we must avoid being *Against Self-Criticism* (2015) as such, for as Freud (1923, p. 51) points out, it would often be a mistake to assume the patient's innocence:

> In certain forms of obsessional neurosis the sense of guilt is over-noisy but cannot justify itself to the ego. Consequently the patient's ego rebels against the imputation of guilt and seeks the physician's support in repudiating it. It would be folly to acquiesce in this, for to do so would have no effect. Analysis eventually shows that the superego is being influenced by processes that have remained unknown to the ego. It is possible to discover the repressed impulses which are really at the bottom of the sense of guilt. Thus in this case the superego knew more than the ego about the unconscious id.

These matters are very complex: sometimes the patient is guiltier than he knows, sometimes more innocent. Careful, discerning analytic inquiry is needed.

For those struggling with existential *angst* I recommend, in addition to getting personal analysis, seeking meaning in trying to be a better person, facing and battling your faults, even getting your mind off yourself long enough to consider that other people might be real and have needs and sufferings you might help to relieve. But for others, those chronically crucifying themselves, it is a matter of helping them climb down from the cross and stand up to their accusers and tormentors.

It is very difficult to get this right. We continually err one way or the other and need to be monitoring ourselves and self-correcting on an ongoing basis. Thanks to Freud's regrettable decision to fold conscience into the superego, we have lost touch with this crucial distinction. People who are out of synch with their conscience are fodder for the persecutory superego, which will generate, one way or another, the physical, mental, and social pain that serves as the equivalent or substitute for the genuine guilt they will not face. As Lucius Annaeus Seneca (Seneca the Younger) put it, "Let wickedness escape as it may at the bar, it never fails of doing justice upon itself, for every guilty person is his own hangman."

The analyst can either be too "superego-ish" with guilt-evading patients or insufficiently confronting, even colluding or turning a blind eye to corruption. We fear being accused of being moralistic or being duped. Plus, like our patients, like everyone else in the culture of narcissism – like everyone else, period – we are reluctant to face our own seamy side. I don't say "dark" side for that sounds sufficiently grand to be almost acceptable. Like Nietzsche's (1883) *Zarathustra* we can accept being great sinners, just not the petty and pathetic creatures we often are. Analysts are not inclined to help patients confront and rise above failings they have not managed to face or deal with in themselves. We know what happens to whistle-blowers in this society. Can you really blow the whistle on others when you have not blown it on yourself and live in dread that someone will?

I write about guilt because I have been struggling with it most of my life. With the help of analysis I have understood that most of my hysterical and psychosomatic symptoms, my anxiety and depression, however grounded in childhood conflicts and pain, has also been rooted in my reactive narcissism, aggression, and wrongdoing. I have had to struggle, and still struggle, to repent and strive to be a better man. With a little progress in this project over the years, my symptoms abated, my creativity was enhanced, and I have been more successful in finding peace and love. There are a lot of fancy psychoanalytic theories that those unready to really face themselves can play around with, but no genuine progress, let alone a cure, will be achieved until they do.

References

Adorno, T. (1983). *Negative Dialectics*. New York: Continuum. (Original work published 1966).

Akhtar, S. (Ed.). (2013). *Guilt: Origins, Manifestations, and Management*. New York: Jason Aronson.

Alexander, F. (1925). A metapsychological description of the process of cure. *International Journal of Psychoanalysis*, 6: 13–34.

Arlow, J. (1982). Problems of the superego concept. *Psychoanalytic Study of the Child*, 37: 229–244.

Bacal, H. A. (1985). Optimal responsiveness and the therapeutic process. In A. Goldberg (Ed.), *Progress in Self Psychology* (pp. 202–226). New York: Guilford.

Barnett, B. (2007). *You Ought To! A Psychoanalytic Study of the Superego and Conscience*. Psychoanalytic Ideas Series (I. Wise and P. Williams, Eds., M. Parsons, Foreword). London: Institute of Psychoanalysis and Karnac Books.

Becker, E. (1973). *The Denial of Death*. New York: Free Press.

Berger, P. (1965). *The Sacred Canopy: A Sociological Theory of Religion*. New York: Doubleday.

Bion, W. R. (1959). Attacks on linking. *International Journal of Psychoanalysis*, 40: 308–315.

Bion, W. R. (1962). *Learning from Experience*. London: Heinemann.

Bion, W. R. (1970). *Attention and Interpretation: A Scientific Approach to Insight in Psycho-Analysis and Groups*. London: Tavistock.

Bloom, P. (2010). The moral life of babies. *New York Times Magazine*, 3 May 2010.

Bloom, P. (2013). *Just Babies: The Origins of Good and Evil*. New York: The Crown Publishing Group.

Bollas, C. (2017). Normotic illness. In *The Shadow of the Object*. New York: Routledge.

Bowlby, J. (1969–1980). *Attachment and Loss,* Vols. 1–3. London: Penguin.

Britton, R. (2003). *Sex, Death, and the Superego: Experiences in Psychoanalysis*. London: Karnac Books.

Buber, M. (1923/1971). *I and Thou*. New York: Scribner's.

Camus, A. (1942). *L'Etranger*. Paris: Gallimard.

Carveth, D. (1984a). Psychoanalysis and social theory. *Psychoanalysis and Contemporary Thought*, 7: 43–98.

Carveth, D. (2010). Superego, conscience and the nature and types of guilt. *Modern Psychoanalysis*, 35(1): 106–130.

Carveth, D. (2012). Freud's and our paranoid myth of "the Beast." *Canadian Journal of Psychoanalysis*, 20(1): 153–157.

Carveth, D. (2013). *The Still Small Voice: Psychoanalytic Reflections on Guilt and Conscience*. London: Karnac.

Carveth, D. (2015). The immoral superego: Conscience as the fourth element in the structural theory of the mind. *Canadian Journal of Psychoanalysis*, 23(1) (Spring, 2015): 206–223.

Carveth, D. (2016). Why we should stop conflating the superego with the conscience. *Psychoanalysis, Culture & Society*, 22(1) (March, 2016): 15–32.

Carveth, D. (2017). Beyond nature and culture: Fromm's existentialism. *Psychoana.l Rev*. 104(4): 485–501.

Carveth, D. (2018). *Psychoanalytic Thinking: A Dialectical Critique of Contemporary Theory and Practice*. London & New York: Routledge.

Carveth, D. & Carveth, J. (2003). Fugitives from guilt: Postmodern de-moralization and the new hysterias. *Am. Imago*, 60: 445–479.

Carveth, D. (2006). Self-punishment as guilt evasion: Theoretical issues. *Canadian Journal of Psychoanalysis*, 14: 172–196.

Carveth, D. (2007). Degrees of Psychopathy vs. "The Psychopath." Comments on J. Reid Meloy's "A Psychoanalytic View of the Psychopath." Presented at the 18th Annual Day in Psychoanalysis, Toronto, April 28th, 2007. Filmed and broadcast by TVOntario; video and audio podcast here: www.tvo.org/TVOsites/WebObjects/ TvoMicrosite.woa?video10149 Summarized as part of a conference report prepared by Prof. William Watson, *Canadian Journal of Psychoanalysis/Revue Canadienne de Psychanalyse* 16(1) (Winter 2008).

Coen, S. (2013). Guilt in therapist and its impact upon treatment. In Akhtar, S. (ed.) (2013), *Guilt: Origins, Manifestations and Management* (pp. 69–82). New York: Jason Aronson.

Collodi, C. (1883). *The Adventures of Pinocchio: Story of a Puppet* (N. J. Perella, Trans.). Berkeley, CA: University of California Press.

De Waal, F. (1997). *Good Natured: The Origins of Right and Wrong in Humans and Other Animals*. Cambridge, MA: Harvard University Press.

Erikson, E. (1950). *Childhood and Society*. New York: Norton.

Esslin, M. (1961). *The Theatre of the Absurd*. New York: Vintage.

Fairbairn, W. R. D. (1952). *An Object Relations Theory of the Personality*. New York: Basic Books.

Ferenczi, S. (1927/1928). The elasticity of psycho-analytic technique. In M. Balint (Ed.), *Final Contributions to the Problems and Methods of Psychoanalysis* (C. Thompson, Intro.), (pp. 87–101). New York: Basic Books.

Fernando, J. (2000). The borrowed sense of guilt. *Int. J. Psycho-Anal.*, 81: 499–512.

Frattaroli, E. (2013). Reflections on the absence of morality in psychoanalytic theory and practice. In S. Akhtar (Ed.) (2013), *Guilt: Origins, Manifestations, and Management* (pp. 83–110). New York: Jason Aronson.

Freud, A. (1936). *The Ego and the Mechanisms of Defence*. New York: International Universities Press.

Freud, S. (1896). The aetiology of hysteria. *S.E.*, 3: 191–221.

Freud, S. (1905). Fragment of an analysis of a case of hysteria. *S.E.*, 7: 1–122.

Freud, S. (1912–1913). Totem and taboo: Some points of agreement between the mental lives of savages and neurotics. *S.E.*, 13: vii–162.

Freud, S. (1914). On narcissism: An introduction. *S.E.*, 14: 67–102.

Freud, S. (1916). Some character-types met with in psycho-analytic work. *S.E.*, 14: 311–333.

Freud, S. (1920). Beyond the pleasure principle. *S.E.*, 18: 1–64.

Freud, S. (1921). Group psychology and the analysis of the ego. *S.E.*, 18: 65–143.

Freud, S. (1923). The ego and the id. *S.E.*, 19: 1–66.

Freud, S. (1930). Civilization and its discontents. *S.E.*, 21: 57–146.

Freud, S. (1933). New introductory lectures on psychoanalysis. *S.E.*, 22: 3–182.

Freud, S. (1940). An outline of psychoanalysis. *S.E.*, 23: 139–208.

Fromm, E. (1947). *Man for Himself: An Inquiry Into the Psychology of Ethics*. New York: Rinehart.

Fromm, E. (1950). *Psychoanalysis and Religion*. New Haven: Yale University Press.

Fromm, E. (1964). *The Heart of Man: Its Genius for Good and Evil*. New York: Harper & Row.

Girard, R. (1989). *The Scapegoat*. Baltimore: Johns Hopkins University Press.

Gray, P. (1994/2005). *The Ego and Analysis of Defense* (2nd ed.). New York: Aronson.

Grinberg, L. (1964). Two kinds of guilt: Their relations with normal and pathological aspects of mourning. *Int. J. Psycho-Anal.*, 45: 366–371.

Hegel, G. W. F. (1807/1977). *Phenomenology of Spirit* (A. V. Miller, Trans.). Oxford: Clarendon.

Hughes, J. (1989). *Reshaping the Psychoanalytic Domain: The Work of Melanie Klein, W. R. D. Fairbairn, and D. W. Winnicott.* Berkeley, CA: University of California Press.

Hughes, J. (2008). *Guilt and Its Vicissitudes: Psychoanalytic Reflections on Morality.* London: Routledge.

Hugo, V. (1862). Les Misérables. In *The Complete Works of Victor Hugo (1802–1885)* (I. F. Hapgood, Trans.). Delphi Classics. www.delphiclassics.com.

Hume, D. (1739–1740). *A Treatise of Human Nature: Being an Attempt to Introduce the Experimental Method of Reasoning into Moral Subjects.* www.gutenberg.org/ebooks/4705.

Hume, D. (1748). *An Inquiry Concerning Human Understanding.* www.gutenberg.org/ebooks/9662.

Jacobson, E. (1964). *The Self and the Object World.* New York: International Universities Press.

Jacoby, R. (1975). *Social Amnesia: A Critique of Contemporary Psychology from Adler to Laing.* Boston: Beacon.

Jaspers, K. (1947). *The Question of German Guilt* (E. B. Ashton, Trans.). New York: Capricorn.

Jung, C. G. (1958/1964). A psychological view of conscience. In *Collected Works of C.G. Jung*, 10: 437–455. Princeton, N.J.: Princeton University Press.

Kant, I. (1785/1993). *Grounding for the Metaphysics of Morals* (3rd ed., J. W. Ellington, Trans.). Indianapolis, IN: Hackett.

Kavaler-Adler, S. (2013). *The Anatomy of Regret: From Death Instinct to Reparation and Symbolization through Vivid Case Studies.* London: Karnac.

Kavaler-Adler, S. (2014). *The Klein-Winnicott Dialectic: Transformative New Metapsychology and Interactive Clinical Theory.* London: Karnac.

Kennedy, R. (2022). *The Evil Imagination: Understanding and Resisting Destructive Forces.* Oxfordshire: Phoenix.

Kernberg, O. (1976). *Object-Relations and Clinical Psychoanalysis.* New York: Aronson.

———. (1991). Aggression and love in the relationship of the couple. *J. Amer. Psychoanal. Assn.*, 39: 45–70.

———. (1993). The couple's constructive and destructive superego functions. *J. Amer. Psychoanal. Assn.*, 41: 653–677.

Kierkegaard, S. (1843/1985). *Fear and Trembling* (A. Hannay, Trans.). New York: Penguin.

Kierkegaard, S. (1849/1989). *The Sickness Unto Death* (A. Hannay, Trans.). Harmondsworth & Middlesex: Penguin.

Klein, M. (1940). Mourning and its relation to manic-depressive states. *Int. J. Psycho-Anal.*, 21: 125–153.

Klein, M. (1946). Notes on some schizoid mechanisms. *Int. J. Psycho-Anal.*, 27: 99–110.

Klein, M. (1948). A contribution to the theory of anxiety and guilt. *Int. J. Psycho-Anal.*, 29: 114–123.

Klein, M. (1952). The origins of transference. *Int. J. Psycho-Anal.*, 33: 433–438.

Klein, M., Heimann, P., Isaacs, S., & Rivière, J. (1952). *Developments in Psychoanalysis*. London: Hogarth.

Kohut, H. (1977). *The Restoration of the Self*. New York: International Universities Press.

Lasch, C. (1979). *The Culture of Narcissism: American Life in an Age of Diminishing Expectations*. New York: Norton.

Lidz, T., Fleck, S., & Cornelison, A. (1965). *Schizophrenia and the Family*. New York: International Universities Press.

Lifton, R. J. (1986). *The Nazi Doctors: Medical Killing and the Psychology of Genocide*. New York: Basic Books.

Marcuse, H. (1970). The obsolescence of the Freudian concept of man. In JJ Shapiro & S.M. Weber (Trans.), *Five Lectures: Psychoanalysis, Politics and Utopia*. Boston: Beacon Press, chapter three, pp. 44–61.

McDougall, J. (1993). *Plea for a Measure of Abnormality*. New York: International Universities Press.

McGlaughlin, N. (2023). *Erich Fromm and Global Public So Iology*. Bristol: Bristol University Press.

Mead, G. H. (1937). *Mind, Self and Society*. Chicago: University of Chicago Press.

Menninger, K. (1938). *Man Against Himself*. New York: Harvest.

Mills, C. Wright. (1959). *The Sociological Imagination*. New York: Oxford University Press.

Milgram, S. (1963). Behavioral study of obedience. *Journal of Abnormal and Social Psychology*, 67: 371–378.

Nash, W. M. (2012). Moral injury in the context of war (research). Workshop Session 508 at the National Zarrow Mental Health Symposium & Mental Health America Annual Conference, 20 September, Tulsa, OK.

Nietzsche, F. (1883/1978). *Thus Spake Zarathustra* (W. Kaufman, Trans.). New York: Penguin.

Nietzsche, F. (1887). *On the Genealogy of Morals: A Polemical Tract*. Second Essay, "Guilt, Bad Conscience and Related Matters." Accessed online at: http://records.viu.ca/~johnstoi/nietzsche/genealogy2.htm See also Kaufmann, W. (1967) (Ed. & Trans.). *On the Genealogy of Morals*. New York: Vintage, pp. 62–63. I find Kaufman's translation less felicitous than the etext version prepared by Ian Johnston.

Pascal, B. (1669/1995). *Pensées and Other Writings*. New York: Oxford University Press.

Phillips, A. (2015). Against self-criticism. *London Review of Books*, 37(5).

Plato (380 BCE). (1974). *Republic* (G. M. A. Grube, Trans.). New York: Hackett Classic.

Racker, H. (1957). The meanings and uses of countertransference. *Psychoanalytic Quarterly*, 26: 303–357.

Rangell, L. (1980). *The Mind of Watergate: An Exploration of the Compromise of Integrity*. New York: W. W. Norton.

Reik, T. (1948/1972). *Listening with the Third Ear*. New York: Arena.

Reiner, A. (2009). *The Quest for Conscience and the Birth of the Mind* (J. Grotstein, Foreword). London: Karnac.

Richards, A. (2014). Contribution to the *Clio's Psyche* psychohistory listserv, 23 June.

Rousseau, J. J. (1754/2010). *Discourse on Inequality*. Whitefish, MT: Kessinger Legacy Reprints.

Sagan, E. (1988). *Freud, Women and Morality: The Psychology of Good and Evil*. New York: Basic Books.

Sandler, J. (1960). On the concept of the superego. *Psychoanalytic Study of the Child*, 15: 128–162.

Schafer, R. (1960). The loving and beloved superego in Freud's structural theory. *Psychoanalytic Study of the Child*, 15: 163–188.

Searles, H. (1975). The patient as therapist to his analyst. In H. Searles (Ed.), *Countertransference and Related Subjects: Selected Papers* (pp. 380–459). New York: International Universities Press. (Original work published 1979).

Shengold, L. (1989). *Soul Murder: The Effects of Childhood Abuse and Deprivation*. New Haven, CT: Yale University Press.

Singletary, W. (2013). Pinocchio's Journey to a 'Good Heart'. In Akhtar, S. (ed.) (2013), *Guilt: Origins, Manifestations and Management* (pp. 15–28). New York: Jason Aronson.

Stoller, R. (1975). *Perversion: The Erotic Form of Hatred*. New York: Pantheon.

———. (1979). *Sexual Excitement*. New York: Pantheon.

———. (1985). *Observing the Erotic Imagination*. New Haven: Yale Univ. Press.

Strachey, J. (1934). The nature of the therapeutic action of psycho-analysis. *International Journal of Psychoanalysis*, 15: 127–159.

Summers, F. (2001). What I do with what you give me: Therapeutic action as the creation of meaning. *Psychoanalytic Psychology*, 18: 635–655.

Symington, N. (1994). *Emotion and Spirit*. London: Karnac.

Twain, M. (1885/2005). *The Adventures of Huckleberry Finn*. Raleigh, NC: Hayes Barton Press.

Untied States Senate Archives (June 9, 1954). Have You No Sense of Decency? Online: www.senate.gov/about/powers-procedures/investigations/mccarthy-hearings/have-you-no-sense-of-decency.htm.

Ury, C. (1998). The Nietzschean monster: Reconsidering guilt in developmental theory. *Canadian Journal of Psychoanalysis*, 6: 51–74.

Westerink, N. (2005/2013). *A Dark Trace: Sigmund Freud on the Sense of Guilt*. Leuven, Belgium: Leuven University Press. Translation from the Dutch: Language Centre, University of Groningen.

Winnicott, D. W. (1965a). Ego distortion in terms of true and false self. In *The Maturational Processes and the Facilitating Environment: Studies in the Theory of Emotional Development*. London: Hogarth Press.

Winnicott, D. W. (1965b). The development of the capacity for concern. In *The Maturational Processes and the Facilitating Environment* (pp. 73–82). London: Hogarth.

Wrong, D. H. (1961). The oversocialized conception of man in modern sociology. *American Sociological Review*, 26: 183–193. Reprinted together with a "Postscript 1975" in Wrong, D. H. (1976). *Skeptical Sociology* (pp. 31–54).

Wurmser, L. (1998). "The sleeping giant": A dissenting comment about "borderline pathology." *Psychoanalytic Inquiry*, 8: 373–397.

Young-Bruehl, E. (2012). *Childism: Confronting Prejudice Against Children*. New Haven, CT: Yale University Press.

Index

Adorno, Theodor 25
aggressive impulse 18, 21, 31, 46
Akhtar, Salman 55–56
Alexander, Franz 25–26, 30, 31,
          40, 43–44
altruism 63
angst 66
animality 14, 22, 24, 40
anxiety: depressive 3, 56, 62–63;
          guilt substitute 2, 35, 51,
          55; persecutory 53, 59,
          65, 67; social 42
Arlow, Jacob 13
Assange, Julian 16–17
authority 9–10, 17, 26, 29–30,
          32, 49

Bacal, Howard A. 14
Barnett, Bernard 41–45
Becker, Ernest 65
Berger, Peter 8, 65
Bion, Wilfred 5, 9, 14, 26, 31,
          40–41, 45–46, 48–49
bisexual 37
blaming 12, 47, 54, 65; *see also*
          victim–blaming
borrowed guilt 5, 14
Bowlby, John 53
Britton, Ronald 30–31
Buber, Martin 60–62

Camus, Albert 12, 16
castration 40, 59
censorship 17
character flaws 66
classism 17, 23, 42
collective guilt 6
complexity 30, 36, 46, 66
compromise of integrity 16–17
condemn 17, 23, 28
conscience: authority 9–10,
          17, 26, 29–30, 32,
          49; defence against
          16–17; development of
          19; good/bad 56, 60;
          grounded in love 26–27,
          32; reconciliation 52;
          repression 16; roots of
          7–9, 31, 39, 43, 62; vs
          superego 21, 32, 42;
          voice of 10, 42, 43, 56
consciousness: of guilt 2, 4;
          higher/lower 62
consequences 26, 27, 40, 55, 61
crime 2–3, 5, 11, 66

death: camp 15, 24; denial of
          65–66; drive 21, 31–32,
          52–53; instinct 24, 51, 53
debt 1, 58
defect 3, 42

defence mechanism 3, 25, 52,
        57–58, 66
delinquency 11
depression: guilt substitute 2,
        15, 36–38; low-grade
        37; parental 54–55;
        unresolved 65
deregulation 13, 16

education 11
egotist 65
empathy 43, 49, 58–59, 62
enlightenment 7, 46
envy 4, 18, 58–59, 66
Eros see life-drive
evil 5, 24, 44–47
existential guilt 5, 47

Fairbairn, Ronald D. 5, 41, 44,
        47–48, 51–51, 54
Ferenczi, Sándor 25–30, 31, 40, 43
Fernando, Joseph 5, 14
fragmentation of self 16
Frattaroli, Elio 55, 60–62
Freud, Sigmund: feminine
        devaluation 27–28, 39;
        guilt, recognition of
        2–3; superego 7, 9, 21,
        23–26, 29; theory of
        psychoanalysis 11, 18
Fromm, Erich 31, 45

Gray, Paul 29
greed 4, 37, 66
Greenspan, Alan 15
guilt: consciousness of 2;
        existential 5, 27, 38, 47,
        66; experiential 1; sense
        of 2, 11, 19, 41, 47, 66;
        unconscious 2–5, 11–12,
        18; useless/harmful
        emotion 2
guilt-substitute 2, 18
Guilty Man 12, 15, 29

hate 4, 9, 28, 32, 40, 49, 57
Hegel, Georg Wilhelm Friedrich 8

heterosexism 17, 23, 38, 40, 42, 65
homosexual 36–37
Hughes, Judith 48–50
Hugo, Victor 22
humanities 18
Hume, David 26

immorality 15, 23–24, 42, 61
incest 21, 23
induced guilt 5, 14, 66
infant: object attachment 31, 39,
        46, 53, 58; research 9, 39
injustice 12, 17, 47
innocent 1, 66
innovation 48
intellect 27, 48

Jacoby, Russell 13
Jaspers, Karl 6
jealousy 58
judge/judgement 1, 8, 17, 30, 35
Jung, Carl Gustav 8, 21, 45
justified: anxiety 50; guilt 4,
        57–58

Kant, Immanuel 31
Kavaler-Adler, Susan 51–55
Kernberg, Otto 18
Kierkegaard, Søren 4, 5, 10
Klein, Melanie 2–5, 9, 16, 24,
        30–32, 39, 41, 44–45,
        48–54, 60, 62
Kleinian insight 13, 39, 48–51, 52,
        56–58
Kohut, Heinz 12, 14, 29, 52
Kristeva, Julia 44

Lasch, Christopher 12
liberal 16, 43
life-drive 21, 28, 31–32, 51
Lifton, Robert J. 24, 40, 44
love, feelings of 32, 36, 45, 50
lust 4

Mahler, Margaret S. 51–51, 55
Manning, Chelsea 16
masochism 2, 13–14, 25, 30

mature development (superego) 24, 27, 33, 46
mature guilt 2, 12, 19
Mead, George Herbert 62
Menninger, Karl 14
Milgram, Stanley 44
misdemeanor 66
moral: behaviour 43; compass 61; conflict `7, 21, 2230; confusion 47; development 49–50, 62; failings 66; law 49; masochism 13–14; norm 1, 30; relativism 31, 49
morality: absence of 55; projection of 22, 31; true 40; understanding of 11, 17, 48

narcissistic: guilt 2, 57–58; pathology 48, 50; personality 2–3, 12–13, 58
neglect 14, 39, 50, 58, 65
neoliberal 13, 16
neurosis 16, 66
new hysterias 15
Nietzsche, Friedrich 1, 5, 18, 45, 67
norms: cultural 9; internalized 7–8, 21, 23, 33; moral 1, 7–8, 21, 32; social 7

obedience 9, 44
Oedipal development 49
Oedipus complex 39

paranoid-schizoid 13, 39, 62
Pascal, Blaise 26, 43
pathology 17–18, 44, 48, 50, 53–54
persecutory guilt: differentiating 24, 55; self-serving 2–3, 39
perspective 2, 11, 47, 50, 51, 57
phantasies 4, 37, 46, 54
Plato 7
politically incorrect 17
pre-Oedipal phase 31, 39, 41, 43

primitive guilt 2, 5, 43, 50
projection 2, 19, 53, 55, 66
psychoanalysis: compromised integrity 16–17; contemporary 52, 54–55; demoralizing , 8; formation and practice 11, 19, 31, 60–61; Freud, father of 48; superego 12–13, 16, 27–28, 30
psychopath 16, 24, 27, 40, 44, 62
psychopathology 3, 18, 24, 29, 42, 51, 56
psychosomatic symptoms 2, 11, 65, 67
PTSD (post-traumatic stress disorder) 9
punishment: fear of 60 (*see also* self–punishment); need for 2, 11, 18–19

racism 17, 23, 42
racist 22–24, 30, 40, 65
Racker, Heinrich 5, 15
Rand, Ayn 16
Rangell, Leo 16
rational: ego 5, 26, 31, 40, 43; judgement 4
rationalism 26, 40, 43, 46, 48
Reagan, Ronald 16
Reflections on the Absence of Morality in Psychoanalytic Theory and Practice (Frattaroli) 15, 60
Reiner, Annie 26, 45–47
relations: I-it/I-thou 52; object 12, 22, 26, 48
remorse 49, 55, 60, 62
reparative guilt: capacity for concern 24, 48; as good guilt 55–56, 60; as mature 2, 13; prosocial 3
repression 2, 16–17, 19, 38, 55
reproach 5, 15, 17, 66
respect 8, 23–24, 26, 50, 61
Richards, Arnold 52

right from wrong 4, 7, 49
Rousseau, Jean-Jacques 26, 40,
        43, 50

sado-masochistic 57–58
Sagan, Eli 9, 22, 26–27, 31,
        39–47, 59
Sandler, Joseph 12
schadenfreude 66
Schafer, Roy 24–25, 50
Searles, Harold 46
seduction theory 5, 14
self-defeat 2, 14, 57
self-harm 2, 13
self-obsession 3, 13
self-punishment 3–4, 13, 25, 30, 36
self-sabotage 2, 18, 30, 66
self-scanning 60, 62
self-torment 2, 39
sex: drive 18, 32; life 36–37
sexist 30, 40, 65
sexual: abuse 14, 61; boundary
        60–61; development
        62; gratification 61;
        impulse 21; inhibition 41;
        repression 38
sexuality 17
shame 3, 13, 16, 37, 39, 52, 55, 61
sins 2–3, 8, 11
Snowden, Edward 16–17
social: authority 49; justice
        warriors 15, 18; norms 7;
        science 7–8, 18
sociopath 17
Sophocles 8

soul 7, 17, 23, 24, 60
Stoller, Robert 18
Strachey, James 28, 28
Summers, Frank 46
superego: critical 15, 18, 35, 66;
        Freudian 16, 39, 56,
        61; grounded in fear of
        rejection 49; internalized
        4; modification 25, 27,
        30, 31, 43; persecutory
        67; as Pop 29; sadistic
        15, 18–19, 24, 42, 51, 57;
        theory of 29, 39, 42
Symington, Neville 45

temptation 59
terror management 65
Thanatos see death drive
Thatcher, Margaret 16
therapeutic action 62
Tragic Man 12, 15, 19
transgression 1–2, 18, 21
Trump, Donald 17
Twain, Mark 9, 22, 40

unconscious guilt 2–5, 11–12, 18
unjustified guilt 4, 51, 66

victim-blaming 5, 14

Westerink, Herman 41
Winnicott 3, 10, 24, 41, 44, 47–48,
        51–52, 60–62
wrongdoing 3, 6, 25, 67
Wurmser, Leon 13